The LACY KNITTING of Mary Schiffmann

NANCY NEHRING

KNITTING AND CHARTS BY PAT SHANNON

INTERWEAVE PRESS

Cover design, Susan Wasinger
Photography, Joe Coca

Interweave Press
201 East Fourth Street
Loveland, Colorado 80537
USA

Printed in the United States by Hart Graphics.

Library of Congress Cataloging-in-Publication Data

Schiffmann, Mary.
    The lacy knitting of Mary Schiffmann / by Nancy Nehring [as told
by Mary Schiffmann].
        p.   cm.
    Includes index.
    ISBN 1-883010-42-X
    1. Knitting. 2. Knitted lace —Patterns. 3. Schiffmann, Mary—Anecdotes.
I. Nehring, Nancy. II. Title.
TT820.S29 1998   97-53191
746.2'2—dc21   CIP

First printing:IWP—7.5M:298:HG

The LACY KNITTING
of Mary Schiffmann

To a kindred soul, Gracie Larsen. Gracie knew the right people necessary to help make Mary's lacy dreams come true.

CONTENTS

INTRODUCTION

I first met Mary Schiffmann in 1994 at a meeting of the Lacy Knitters, a group she cofounded to promote lace knitting by collecting, cataloging, and making available old knitted lace patterns. Mary had collected more than 500 patterns in her lifetime and these form the foundation of the Lacy Knitters pattern bank. At the time we met, Mary no longer knitted herself—her hands weren't steady enough—but she could still explain how to work a stitch, translate an unfamiliar term from an old pattern, and make us laugh with her wry sense of humor.

Mary's joy was collecting patterns. While she did make doilies, she rarely made garments. Often she knitted only a tiny swatch, maybe only an inch or two of an edging. Sometimes she didn't even do that; she just wrote out the pattern, never proofknitting it at all. Mary could "see" the knitting in her head.

The patterns that she did knit up, such as Heirloom Apron Lace for pillowcase edgings, went through many changes. Mary was constantly trying out new ideas, combining different stitches and modifying patterns. Knitting was not static to her.

When reminiscing about her pattern collecting, Mary commented that doilies have always been knitted from a written pattern. The patterns are too complicated to keep in one's head. But edging patterns, being simpler, have frequently been passed from person to person via a swatch. Well into this century, most knitters could copy the stitches, or a close approximation, from a tiny swatch. Sometimes these swatches were made into samplers similar to embroidery samplers or gathered into swatch books as crochet patterns often were.

Mary had a definite way of doing things. She invariably used Knit-Cro-Sheen and size 1 needles to knit her doilies. During the 1940s, 50s, and 60s, when Mary did much of her knitting, there was little demand for specialized lace-knitting supplies. But every dime store carried Knit-Cro-Sheen, so that's what she used for her doilies. And size 1 needles were used for gloves and baby clothing, both still frequently knitted at home and therefore available. Mary felt that finer crochet threads made a doily that was hard to iron out because it balled up when washed. For edgings, Mary usually used size 50-30 crochet thread on size 0 needles.

Many patterns in this book use thread and/or needle sizes different from Mary's standbys. Nowadays, more threads, with varying properties, are available. Cordonnet is tightly twisted and does not ball up even when sizes as small as 30 are used for doilies. And larger needles relative to the size of the thread have opened up several of the patterns, giving a more lacy look.

Mary did not block her knitting but ironed it out. Household laces were used to protect fine wood furniture from dents and scratches or to trim linens so ironing them out was a lot less time consuming than blocking. Today knitted laces are displayed for their intricate beauty alone, so blocking, which emphasizes the pattern and symmetry, is more common. And Mary, more than any other person I know, appreciated that beauty.

Mary very much wanted to see her collection of patterns in print. She felt like a lone crusader in the 1950s, 60s, and 70s as she watched interest in lace knitting die. To her, a book would preserve patterns in a form usable to others, and Mary helped select a number of the patterns presented here. One of my few regrets in knowing Mary is that she did not get to see this book published.

Mary was constantly on the lookout for unusual knitting. She was always willing to look at any knitted piece she hadn't seen before, but much of what she saw she dismissed as "standard". Standard patterns to her were ones that combined the easy, the common, or the frequently published. In an attempt to convey Mary's appreciation of knitted lace, I've omitted all standard patterns and basic how-to-knit instructions here. Although I've included a few easy but unusual patterns, most require intermediate to advanced knitting skills.

Mary died April 28, 1996. Her last words to her knitting friends were, "I spent my life looking for patterns. Don't you quit."

KNITTED WASHCLOTHS

I was born on March 12, 1908 in Kobe, Japan. My first memories of knitting were in 1914 when I was six years old. The Red Cross was asking for knitters to outfit "the boys in the trenches." We even heard about the request in Japan where my parents were missionaries. Since no Japanese could knit (as far as we knew), it was up to those who could, like my mother.

The first material we received was gauze, one foot wide. We tore it into strips three inches wide and wound them for bandages. Since the selvedge would have been harsh on wounds, we tore them off and knitted them into washcloths. Making these washcloths was how I learned to knit.

Later, real yarn arrived. Mother knitted fifty pairs of socks—as well as sweaters, gloves, and airmen's helmets. The airmen's helmets were the prototypes of ski masks and were so complicated that even Mother had trouble with them. It was no blow to my pride to be told they were too difficult for me! The war in Europe ended in 1918, but it continued in Siberia between the Reds and the Whites, so we kept on knitting until we came home to America in 1919.

Mother would read to us children as she knitted. She couldn't do heels and toes while reading though; she had to concentrate on those parts. She read anything appropriate for children. I remember the Jeeves books.

Warren family passport photo, circa 1928. Left to right: Charles (younger brother), Mary, Janet (younger sister), Dana (older brother), Cora (Mother), and Charles (Father).

11

Mother's Handkerchief Edging

Created for Mother circa 1953.

Finished size: Depth ¾", repeat interval ¾".
Yarn: DMC Cebelia 30 (100% cotton; 520m/50g): white.
Needles: Size 1 (2.4 mm).

CO 6 sts. Knit 1 row.
Row 1: K1, yo, p2tog, k2tog, k1— 5 sts.
Row 2: Yo, k2, yo, p2tog, k1— 6 sts.
Row 3: K1, yo, p2tog, k1, yo, k2— 7 sts.
Row 4: Yo, k4, yo, p2tog, k1—8 sts.
Row 5: K1, yo, p2tog, k3, yo, k2— 9 sts.
Row 6: Yo, k2tog twice, k2, yo, p2tog, k1—8 sts.
Row 7: K1, yo, p2tog, k2, k2tog, k1—7 sts.
Row 8: Yo, k2tog twice, yo, p2tog, k1—6 sts.
Repeat Rows 1–8 for length desired.

Repeat from Row 1 for length desired.

CO 6 sts. Knit 1 row.

WALKER MISSIONARY HOME

When my parents returned to Japan in 1921, I stayed at the Walker Missionary Home, Auburndale, Massachusetts, to complete high school. The home was a school mostly for missionary children (today it is a retirement home for former missionaries). The third floor was for boys, the second floor was for families, and the back of the first floor was for girls. We high-schoolers would take the cart from the eighth-grade room to the hill out back. We would take turns getting on and riding down the first hill, then up the next hill and down, then up a third and down.

Mary at Walker Missionary Home about 1921.

Diamond Doily

This is a short row or "gore" doily. There is no center start and it is knitted with only two needles.

Finished size: 13 ½" diameter.
Yarn: Lanas Stop, Algodon Egipcio No. 8 (100% cotton; 712m/100g): white, 1 ball.
Needles: Size 2 (2.8 mm).
Notions: Size 22 tapestry needle.

CO 50 sts using a provisional cast-on (see page 15). Purl 1 row.

Row 1: K6, yo, k2tog, k3, yo, sl 2 tog k-wise, k1, p2sso, yo, k3, k2tog, yo, k5, yo, k2tog, k3, yo, sl 2 tog k-wise, k1, p2sso, yo, k16, turn—2 sts rem.
Row 2 and all even rows: Sl 1, p to 4 sts from end, k4.
Row 3: K9, k2tog, yo, k3, yo, k2tog, k1, k2tog, yo, k5, yo, k2tog, k1, k2tog, yo, k3, yo, k2tog, k12, turn—4 sts rem.
Row 5: K6, yo, (k2tog twice, yo, k5, yo) 3 times, k2tog, k9, turn—6 sts rem.

Row 7: K9, yo, k2tog, k3, k2tog, yo, k1, k2tog, yo, k5, yo, k2tog, k1, yo, k2tog, k3, k2tog, yo, k8, turn—8 sts rem.
Row 9: K6, yo, k2tog, k2, yo, k2tog, k1, k2tog, yo, k2, k2tog, yo, k5, yo, k2tog, k2, yo, k2tog, k1, k2tog, yo, k7, turn—10 sts rem.
Row 11: K11, yo, sl 2 tog k-wise, k1, p2sso, yo, k3, k2tog, yo, k5, yo, k2tog, k3, yo, sl 2 tog k-wise, k1, p2sso, yo, k6, turn—12 sts rem.

Diamond Doily.

Mary's Teaching Notes
Kitchener Stitch

1. Bring yarn needle through the first front st as if to purl, leaving the st on needle.

2. Bring yarn needle through the first back st as if to knit, and then sl this st off needle. Bring yarn needle through next back st as if to purl, leaving the st on needle.

3. Bring yarn needle through the same front st as if to knit, and then sl this st off needle. Bring needle through the next front st as if to purl, again leaving the st on needle.

4. Bring yarn needle through the first back st as if to purl, sl that st off, and then bring yarn needle through the next back st as if to knit, leaving it on needle. Rep steps 3 and 4 until no sts remain.

Row 13: K6, yo, k2tog, k1, k2tog, yo, k3, yo, k2tog, k1, k2tog, yo, k5, yo, k2tog, k1, k2tog, yo, k3, yo, k2tog, k2, turn—14 sts rem.

Row 15: K8, k2tog, (yo, k5, yo, k2tog twice) 2 times, yo, k6, turn—16 sts rem.

Row 17: K6, yo, k2tog, k1, yo, k2tog, k3, k2tog, yo, k1, k2tog, yo, k5, yo, k2tog, k1, yo, k2tog, k3, turn—18 sts rem.

Row 19: K10, yo, k2tog, k1, k2tog, yo, k2, k2tog, yo, k5, yo, k2tog, k2, yo, k2tog, turn—20 sts rem.

Row 21: K6, yo, k2tog, k3, yo, sl 2 tog k-wise, k1, p2sso, yo, k3, k2tog, yo, k5, yo, k2tog, k2, turn—22 sts rem.

> *Mary's Teaching Notes*
> ## Provisional Cast On
>
> With a crochet hook, make a loose chain as many stitches long as you need to cast on. If you examine the chain, you will notice that two threads form a V on the front and a third thread on the back is straight. Working through the back thread only, pick up a stitch with your knitting needle. When you have completed your knitting, pull on the tail of the chain stitch, pulling out one chain at a time, and graft the two knitted edges together.

Numbers in blank squares indicate number of stitches remaining at the turn. Repeat pattern 11 times. Graft first and last rows together.

(Knitting chart, rows 1–48, 50 stitches wide)

All even rows: S1 1, p to within 4 sts of end, k4.

CO 50 sts using provisional cast-on. Purl 1 row.

Row 23: K9, k2tog, yo, k3, yo, k2tog, k1, k2tog, yo, k5, yo, k2tog, turn—24 sts rem.

Row 25: K6, (yo, k2tog twice, yo, k5) 2 times, turn—26 sts rem.

Row 27: K9, yo, k2tog, k3, k2tog, yo, k1, k2tog, yo, k3, turn—28 sts rem.

Row 29: K6, yo, k2tog, k2, yo, k2tog, k1, k2tog, yo, k2, k2tog, yo, k1, turn—30 sts rem.

Row 31: K11, yo, sl 2 tog k-wise, k1, p2sso, yo, k4, turn—32 sts rem.

Row 33: K6, yo, k2tog, k1, k2tog, yo, k3, yo, k2tog, turn—34 sts rem.

Row 35: K8, k2tog, yo, k4, turn—36 sts rem.

Row 37: K6, (yo, k2tog, k1) twice, turn—38 sts rem.

Row 39; K10, turn—40 sts rem.

Row 41: K6, yo, k2tog, turn—42 sts rem.

Row 43: K6, turn—44 sts rem.

Row 45: K4, turn—46 sts rem.

Row 47: K50.

Row 48: Sl 1, p45, k4.
Repeat pattern for a total of 11 gores.

Finishing: Using the kitchener stitch (see page 14), graft the first and last rows together. To make the center hole smaller, pick up the slipped stitches in the center of the doily, run a thread through, and tighten.

Mt. Holyoke

My grandmother, mother, and four of my five aunts all attended Mt. Holyoke College in South Hadley, Massachusetts. My grandmother was there the last year Mary Lyon was. Mary Lyon was the founding president and the last president who could substitute-teach in any class.

I received my B.A. in English literature from Mt. Holyoke. Then I attended Boston University and received an M.A. in education in 1929. I did student teaching, but couldn't maintain any discipline in class, so I had to give that up.

After graduating, I worked at any job I could get until I married in 1944. I worked as a housekeeper, cook, bookkeeper, and credit union manager.

Zigzag Doily

This is a short row or "gore" doily adapted from "The Story of American Needlework" in Woman's Day, 1961. I incorporated a separate "to-be-sewn-on" edging into the doily pattern.

Finished size: 15" diameter.

Yarn: DMC Cebelia 10 (100% cotton; 260m/50g): white, 1 ball.
Needles: Size 2 (2.8 mm).
Notions: Size 22 tapestry needle.

Using a provisional cast-on (see page 15), CO 53 sts. Knit 1 row.

Row 1: Sl 1, k46, yo, k2tog, k2, yo, k2.

Row 2: (K4, yo, k2tog) 3 times, k33, turn—3 sts rem.

Row 3: Sl 1, k43, yo, k2tog, k3, yo, k2.

Row 4: (K5, yo, k2tog) twice, k4, yo, k2tog, k29, turn—6 sts rem.

Row 5: Sl 1, k40, yo, k2tog, (k2, yo) twice, k2.

Row 6: K7, yo, k2tog, k6, yo, k2tog, k4, yo, k2tog, k25, turn—9 sts rem.

Row 7: Sl 1, k37, yo, k2tog, k8.

Row 8: BO 4, k2, yo, k2tog, k7, yo, k2tog, k4, yo, k2tog, k21, turn—12 sts rem.

Row 9: Sl 1, k34, yo, k2tog, k2, yo, k2.

Row 10: K4, yo, k2tog, k2, ssk, yo, (k1, yo, k2tog) 2 times, k4, yo, k2tog, k17, turn—15 sts rem.

Row 11: Sl 1, k31, yo, k2tog, k3, yo, k2.

Row 12: K5, yo, k2tog, k1, ssk, yo, k3, yo, k2tog, k1, yo, k2tog, k4, yo, k2tog, k13, turn—18 sts rem.

Row 13: Sl 1, k28, yo, k2tog, (k2, yo) twice, k2.

Row 14: K7, yo, k2tog, k1, k2tog, yo, k3, yo, ssk twice, yo, k4, ssk, yo, k11, turn—21 sts rem.

Row 15: Sl 1, k25, yo, k2tog, k8.

Row 16: BO 4, k2, yo, k2tog, k3, yo, sl 2 tog k-wise, k1, p2sso, yo, k1, ssk, yo, k4, ssk, yo, k9, turn—24 sts rem.

Row 17: Sl 1, k22, yo, k2tog, k2, yo, k2.

Row 18: K4, yo, k2tog, k6, ssk, yo, k4, ssk, yo, k7, turn—27 sts rem.

Row 19: Sl 1, k19, yo, k2tog, k3, yo, k2.

Row 20: K5, yo, k2tog, k5, ssk, yo, k4, ssk, yo, k5, turn—30 sts rem.

Row 21: Sl 1, k16, yo, k2tog, (k2, yo) 2 times, k2.

Row 22: K7, yo, k2tog, k4, ssk, yo, k4, ssk, yo, k3, turn—33 sts rem.

Row 23: Sl 1, k13, yo, k2tog, k8.

Row 24: BO 4, k2, yo, k2tog, k3, ssk, yo, k4, ssk, yo, k37. Repeat for a total of 19 gores.

Finishing: Using the kitchener stitch (see page 14), graft the first and last rows together. To make the center hole smaller, pick up the slipped stitches in the center of the doily, run a thread through, and tighten.

The numbers appearing in the blank squares indicate number of stitches not worked before turning.

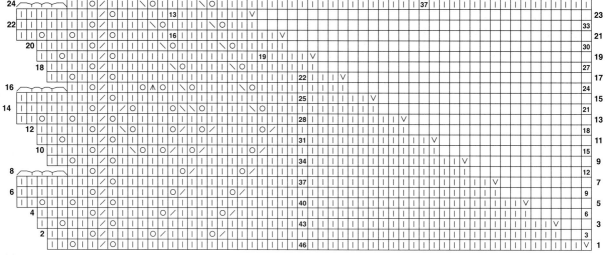

CO 53 sts using provisional cast-on. Knit 1 row.

AUNT JENNIE'S KNITTED LACE

I first heard about lace knitting some seventy-odd years ago because my dear Aunt Jennie (Jennie W. Elston, father's sister) did it. Aunt Jennie lived in the house built by my grandfather Warren in Collinsville, Connecticut. I would visit Aunt Jennie in the summers and see her knitting. She had a big dress box almost full of rolls of knitted lace in pillowcase lengths. These she would put on pillowcases for Christmas presents. She called this type of knitting white knitting.

Jennie knitted baby sweaters and leggings for a store in Brooklyn. This brought in a little pin money.

Fagot and Diamond Edging

Finished size: Depth 2", repeat interval ¾".

Yarn: DMC Cordonnet 30 (100% cotton; 197m/20g): white.
Needles: Size 0 (2.1 mm).

CO 18 sts. Knit 1 row.

Row 1: Sl 1, k1, yo, p2tog, k4, yo, ssk, k3, yo, p2tog, k1, yo twice, k2—20 sts.

Row 2: K3, p1, k1, yo, p2tog, k9, yo, p2tog, k2.

Row 3: Sl 1, k1, yo, p2tog, k3, (yo, ssk) 2 times, k2, yo, p2tog, k5.

Row 4: K5, yo, p2tog, k9, yo, p2tog, k2.

Row 5: Sl 1, k1, yo, p2tog, k2 (yo, ssk) 3 times, k1, yo, p2tog, k5.

Row 6: BO 2, k2, yo, p2tog, k9, yo, p2tog, k2—18 sts.

Row 7: Sl 1, k1, yo, p2tog, k3, (yo, ssk) 2 times, k2, yo, p2tog, k1, yo twice, k2—20 sts.

Mary's Teaching Notes
Fagot Stitch

The dictionary definition of a fagot is a bundle of sticks used for fuel. In knitting, it is a bundle of stitches. In some old directions it is indicated by "yo, p2tog", in others by "f". The method is the same; yo twice, once for the transition to purling, once to leave a yo on the needle; then p2tog. I have tried using k2tog, but it isn't the same. Fagoting can be used to lengthen a pattern to suit a particular need or to add a heading to an edging that doesn't have one. Routinely one has rows of fagots atop each other, as in this sample.

Row 8: K3, p1, k1, yo, p2tog, k9, yo, p2tog, k2.

Row 9: Sl 1, k1, yo, p2tog, k4, yo, ssk, k3, yo, p2tog, k5.

Row 10: K5, yo, p2tog, k9, yo, p2tog, k2.

Row 11: Sl 1, k1, yo, p2tog, k9, yo, p2tog, k5.

Row 12: BO 2, k2, yo, p2tog, k9, yo, p2tog, k2—18 sts.

Repeat Rows 1–12 for length desired.

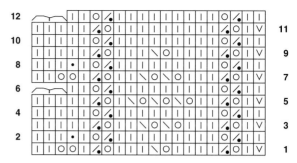

Repeat from Row 1 for length desired.

CO 18 sts. Knit 1 row.

Aunt Jennie's Shark's Tooth Edging

(Shown on page 34.)

Finished size: Depth 2", repeat interval 1".

Yarn: DMC Cordonnet 30 (100% cotton; 197m/20g): white.

Needles: Size 0 (2.1 mm).

CO 15 sts. Knit 1 row.

Row 1: Sl 1, k3, (yo, k2tog) 3 times, k1, yo twice, k2tog, k2—16 sts.

Row 2: K4, p1, k3, (yo, k2tog) 3 times, k2.

Row 3: Sl 1, k3, (yo, k2tog) 3 times, k2, yo twice, k2tog, k2—17 sts.

Row 4: K4, p1, k4, (yo, k2tog) 3 times, k2.

Row 5: Sl 1, k3, (yo, k2tog) 3 times, k3, yo twice, k2tog, k2—18 sts.

Row 6: K4, p1, k5, (yo, k2tog)

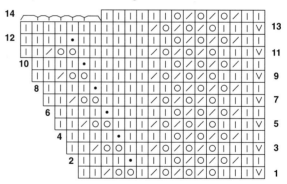

Repeat from Row 1 for length desired.

CO 15 sts. Knit 1 row.

Mary's Teaching Notes
Witches' Ladder
A witches' ladder is similar to a fagot except that it uses a knit stitch: yo, k2tog.

3 times, k2.

Row 7: Sl 1, k3, (yo, k2tog) 3 times, k4, yo twice, k2tog, k2—19 sts.

Row 8: K4, p1, k6, (yo, k2tog) 3 times, k2.

Row 9: Sl 1, k3, (yo, k2tog) 3 times, k5, yo twice, k2tog,

k2—20 sts.

Row 10: K4, p1, k7, (yo, k2tog) 3 times, k2.

Row 11: Sl 1, k3, (yo, k2tog) 3 times, k6, yo twice, k2tog, k2—21 sts.

Row 12: K4, p1, k8, (yo, k2tog) 3 times, k2.

Row 13: Sl 1, k3, (yo, k2tog) 3 times, k11.

Row 14: BO 6, k6, (yo, k2tog) 3 times, k2—15 sts.

Repeat Rows 1–14 for length desired.

THE COLLINSVILLE KNITTERS

In the 1920s, there were four or five women in Collinsville, Connecticut, who shared patterns with names like "Wheel Lace", "Pineapple Lace", "Laura Brown's Rose-Leaf Lace", and "Nellie Latimer's Mother's Lace".

Aunt Jennie kept a notebook of all her patterns.

Many patterns were handwritten on the backs of envelopes or any other scrap of paper that might have been handy. Some patterns are as old as the late 1800s. Luckily, when Aunt Jennie died, I inherited her notebook. I knitted up each pattern and typed the instructions.

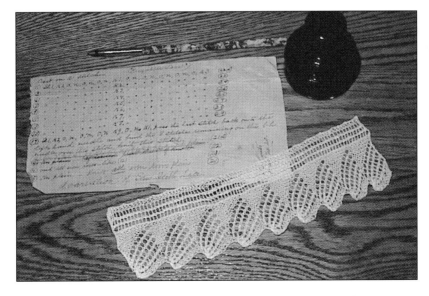

Aunt Jennie's instructions for Pineapple Lace were handwritten on the back of an envelope. This is among the oldest patterns in my collection.

Pineapple Lace

This is a variant of the classic Saw Tooth pattern.

Finished size: Depth 2 ½", repeat interval 1".
Yarn: DMC Cordonnet 30 (100% cotton; 197m/20g): white.
Needles: Size 0 (2.1 mm).

CO 21 sts.

Row 1: Sl 1, k2, (yo, k2tog) 3 times, k1, (yo, ssk) 4 times, yo, k3—22 sts.

Row 2 and all even rows: Knit.

Row 3: Sl 1, k2, (yo, k2tog) 3 times, k2, (yo, ssk) 4 times, yo, k3—23 sts.

Row 5: Sl 1, k2, (yo, k2tog) 3 times, k3, (yo, ssk) 4 times, yo, k3—24 sts.

Row 7: Sl 1, k2, (yo, k2tog) 3 times, k4, (yo, ssk) 4 times, yo, k3—25 sts.

Row 9: Sl 1, k2, (yo, k2tog) 3 times, k5, (yo, ssk) 4 times, yo, k3—26 sts.

Row 11: Sl 1, k2, (yo, k2tog) 3 times, k6, (yo, ssk) 4 times, yo, k3—27 sts.

Row 13: Sl 1, k2, (yo, k2tog) 3 times, k7, (yo, ssk) 4 times, yo, k3—28 sts.

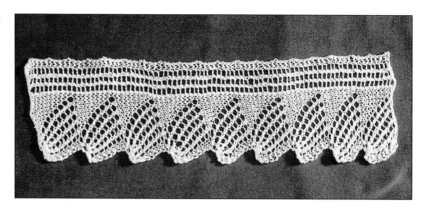

⊡ **Pass the last st back onto the left-hand needle and pass the 8 sts remaining on the left-hand needle over this st. Knit the st.**

Repeat from Row 1 for length desired.

CO 21 sts.
All even rows: Knit.

Mary's Teaching Notes
Easy Sew-on Edging

Always slip first stitch of an edging on the straight edge. On an insertion, slip first stitch on both edges. This makes a little loop so it is easier to sew the edging or insertion onto the fabric. Slip as to knit gives a firm, straight edge. Slip as to purl gives a straight but more flexible edge.

Row 15: Sl 1, k2, (yo, k2tog) 3 times, k8, (yo, ssk) 4 times, yo, k3—29 sts.

Row 17: Sl 1, k2, (yo, k2tog) 3 times, k9, yo, ssk, k1, pass the last st back onto the left needle and pass the 8 sts rem on the left over this st, k the st—21 sts.

Row 18: Knit.

Repeat Rows 1–18 for length desired.

Nellie Latimer's Mother's Lace

Handwritten pattern from Aunt Jennie. Because this lace curves easily, it's a good candidate for a collar or the edging on a fabric-centered doily.

Finished size: Depth 2", repeat interval 1 ½".

Yarn: DMC Cebelia 10 (100% cotton; 260m/50g): color 754.

Needles: Size 2 (2.8 mm).

CO 15 sts. Knit 1 row.

Row 1: Sl 1, k8, p1, yo, k1, yo, p1, k3—17 sts.

Row 2: K4, p3, k3, yo twice, k2tog, k5—18 sts.

Row 3: Sl 1, k6, p1, k2, p1, k1, (yo, k1) 2 times, p1, k3—20 sts.

Row 4: K4, p5, k11.

Row 5: Sl 1, k9, p1, k2, yo, k1, yo, k2, p1, k3—22 sts.

Row 6: K4, p7, k3, (yo twice, k2tog) 2 times, k4—24 sts.

Row 7: Sl 1, k5, (p1, k2) 2 times, p1, k7, p1, k3.

Row 8: K4, p7, k13.

Row 9: Sl 1, k11, p1, ssk, k3, k2tog, p1, k3—22 sts.

Repeat from Row 1 for length desired.

CO 15 sts. Knit 1 row.

Row 10: K4, p5, k2, (yo twice, k2tog) 3 times, k5—25 sts.

Row 11: Sl 1, k6, p1, (k2, p1) 2 times, k1, p1, ssk, k1, k2tog, p1, k3—23 sts.

Row 12: K4, p3, k16.

Row 13: Sl 1, k14, p1, sl 2 tog k-wise, k1, p2sso, p1, k3—21 sts.

Row 14: K21.

Row 15: Sl 1, k20.

Row 16: BO 6, knit 14—15 sts.

Repeat Rows 1–16 for length desired.

Aunt Lucy's Lace

My Aunt Lucy Keith lived in my mother's family home in Braintree, Massachusetts. I found this scrap of lace used to trim curtains among the flotsam and jetsam in an old box of sewing notions. I converted the bobbin-lace pattern to a knit one.

Aunt Lucy gave me some handwritten patterns from her mother.

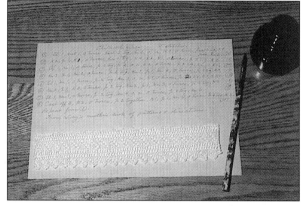

Handwritten pattern for Chillicothe Lace from Aunt Lucy's mother's collection of patterns.

I created Shell Lace by adapting a lace pattern from machine-made bobbin lace. Machine-made lace on top, knitted lace on bottom. The bobbin lace dates from about 1900.

Shell Lace

Finished size: Depth 1 ½", repeat interval 1 ½".

Yarn: DMC Cebelia 30 (100% cotton; 515m/50g): white.

Needles: Size 0 (2.1mm).

CO 19 sts.

Set-up Row A: Sl 1, k1, (yo, k2tog) 8 times, k1—19 sts.

Set-up Row B: Yo, k2tog, knit to end.

Row 1: Sl 1, k1, (yo, k2tog) 3 times, k2tog, (yo, k2tog) 4 times, k1—18 sts.

Row 2 and all even rows: Yo, k2tog, knit to end.

Row 3: Sl 1, k1, (yo, k2tog) 3 times, k1, k2tog, (yo, k2tog) 3 times, k1—17 sts.

Row 5: Sl 1, k1, (yo, k2tog) 3 times, k2, k2tog, (yo, k2tog) 2 times, k1—16 sts.

Row 7: Sl 1, k1, (yo, k2tog) 3 times, k3, k2tog, yo, k2tog, k1—15 sts.

Row 9: Sl 1, k1, (yo, k2tog) 3 times, k4, k2tog, k1—14 sts.

Row 11: Sl 1, k1, (yo, k2tog) 3 times, k4, yo, k2—15 sts.

Row 13: Sl 1, k1, (yo, k2tog) 3 times, k3, yo, k1, yo, k2tog, k1—16 sts.

Row 15: Sl 1, k1, (yo, k2tog) 3 times, k2, yo, k1, (yo, k2tog) 2 times, k1—17 sts.

Row 17: Sl 1, k1, (yo, k2tog) 3 times, k1, yo, k1, (yo, k2tog) 3 times, k1—18 sts.

Row 19: Sl 1, k1, (yo, k2tog) 3 times, yo, k1, (yo, k2tog) 4 times, k1—19 sts.

Row 20: Yo, k2tog, knit to end.

Repeat Rows 1–20 for desired length.

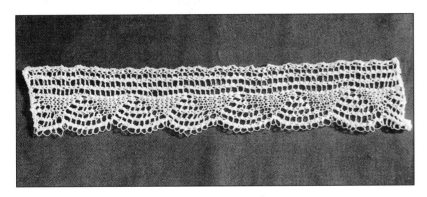

Repeat from Row 1 for length desired.

Row 2 and all even rows: yo, k2tog, knit to end.

CO 19 sts.

Chillicothe Lace

Handwritten pattern from my Aunt Lucy's mother's book of patterns and directions.

Finished size: Depth 1 ¼", repeat ½".

Yarn: DMC Cordonnet 30 (100% cotton; 197m/20g): white.
Needles: Size 0 (2.1 mm).

CO 15 sts. Knit 1 row.
Row 1: Sl 1, k1, yo, p2tog, k1, yo, ssk, k3, yo, p2tog, k1, yo, k2—16 sts.
Row 2: K2, p1, k1, yo, p2tog, k4, p1, k1, yo, p2tog, k2.
Row 3: Sl 1, k1, yo, p2tog, k2, yo, ssk, k2, yo, p2tog, k2, yo, k2—17 sts.
Row 4: K2, p1, k2, yo, p2tog, k3, p1, k2, yo, p2tog, k2.
Row 5: Sl 1, k1, yo, p2tog, k3, yo, ssk, k1, yo, p2tog, k3, yo, k2—18 sts.
Row 6: K2, p1, k3, yo, p2tog, k2, p1, k3, yo, p2tog, k2.
Row 7: Sl 1, k1, yo, p2tog, k4, yo, ssk, yo, p2tog, k6.
Row 8: BO 3, k2, yo, p2tog, k1, p1, k4, yo, p2tog, k2—15 sts.

Repeat Rows 1–8 for length desired.

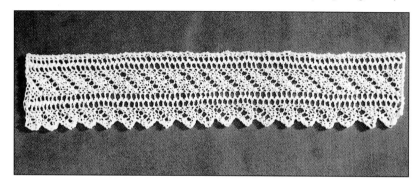

Repeat from Row 1 for length desired.

CO 15 sts. Knit 1 row.

CHARLES KNITS ON SHIP

My mother also taught my brothers to knit. My brother Charles became an ambulance driver in Europe during World War II. He was sent by ship around Cape Horn. He noticed some yarn on board and asked if he could have some to knit with. Other sailors laughed at him until somewhere near Rio de Janeiro when the laughter turned to envy—Charles had something to do on the long trip.

He made a scarf with his initials knitted in and kept it for many years after the war.

Diagonal Check Ground Scarf

Finished size: Repeat width 1", repeat height 1 ¼", block scarf to 10 × 44 inches.

Yarn: Patons, Kroy 4 ply (85% wool, 15% nylon; 1 ¾ oz skein): color 490, 3 skeins.

Needles: Size 4 (3.5mm).

Gauge: 18 sts = 4" (10 cm).

Diagonal Check Ground: Repeat of 8 stitches, 10 rows.

Row 1: P1, yo, ssk, k4, p1.

Row 2 and all even rows: K1, p6, k1.

Row 3: P1, k1, yo, ssk, k3, p1.

Row 5: P1, k2, yo, ssk, k2, p1.

Row 7: P1, k3, yo, ssk, k1, p1.

Row 9: P1, k4, yo, ssk, p1.

Row 10: K1, p6, k1.

•**Scarf:** CO 66 sts. Work garter stitch (knit every row) for 8 rows. Keeping first and last 5 sts in garter stitch, repeat pattern 7 times across. The 10 pattern rows are repeated 37 times, ending with row 9. Garter stitch for 8 rows. BO loosely.

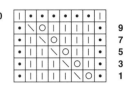

CO 8 sts for each repeat.
Even rows: K1, p6, k1.

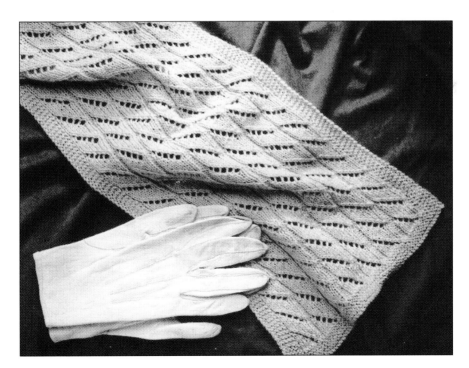

Shocks of Corn Ground Baby Jacket

This is a variation of a standard pattern called Shetland Acre or Plowed Field. Baby jacket is size 3 months.

Finished size: Repeat width 1 ¼", repeat height ½".

Yarn: Unger, Baby Utopia (100% acrylic; 50 g): Color 28, 2 skeins.

Needles: Size 3 (3.2mm).

Notions: 4 stitch holders; for baby jacket—size 18 tapestry needle, ¾ yd ¼" ribbon.

Shocks of Corn Ground: Pattern is multiple of 12 sts + edge sts.

Row 1: Yo, ssk, k5, k2tog, yo, k1, yo, k2tog.

Row 2: P1, yo, p2tog, yo, p1, p2tog tbl, p3, p2tog, p1, yo.

Row 3: Yo, k2, ssk, k1, k2tog, k2, yo, k1, yo, k2tog.

Row 4:. P1, yo, p2tog, yo, p3, p3tog, p3, yo.

Body: CO 164 sts: 40 sts for right front, 84 sts for back, and 40 sts for left front. There are 13 pat-

CO multiple of 12 sts plus edge sts.

28

tern repeats plus 4 edge sts on each side. Keeping first and last four stitches in garter stitch, repeat pattern until piece measures 6 ½ inches (16.5 cm). Divide for fronts and back. Knit, in pattern, 38 sts, slip sts just knit to holder, BO 4 sts for underarm. Knit, in pattern, 80 sts for back, slip remaining 42 sts to holder.

Back: Knit in pattern for 4 inches (10 cm) ending with a wrong-side row.

Shoulders:

Row 1: K28 in pattern, k2tog, BO 20, sl next st then k2 sts on right-hand needle tog, k28 in pattern.

Row 2: P27 in pattern, p2tog.

Row 3: Ssk, k26.

Sl 27 sts just worked to a stitch holder. Repeat for other shoulder, reversing shaping.

Right Front: Pick up 38 front sts from holder. Beg at front edge, knit in pattern until front measures 8 inches (20.5 cm) from the bottom, ending at front edge.

Start neck and shoulder.

Row 1: Beginning at front edge of right front, k4, ssk, k10, cont in patt.

Row 2: Work 22 in pattern, k9, k2tog, k4.

Continue alternating Rows 1 and 2, decreasing 1 st in the garter stitch pattern until there are 30 sts on needle. Knit in pattern with 4 garter stitches at neck edge until the front measures the same as the back. Put 26 sts on one stitch holder and the 4 border sts on another.

Left Front: Beg at sleeve side with RS facing, pick up 42 sts from holder.

Row 1: BO 4 sts, work 22 in patt, k10, k2tog, k4.

Row 2: K4, ssk, k9, cont in patt.

Continue, reversing shaping for right front.

Graft shoulders together using kitchener stitch (see page 14). Keep 4 border sts of each front on holders.

Sleeve: CO 74 sts (6 pattern repeats plus 2 edge sts). K 1 row. K in pattern for 6 inches (15 cm). BO 2 sts at the beginning of the next 2 rows. BO rem sts. Sew underarm seams. Insert sleeve into body armhole and sew. Make 2.

Neck: Take 4 garter sts from holder. Continue knitting garter sts until strip meets center back, put on holder. Repeat for other side. Sew strips to neck edge, grafting sts together at center back.

Finishing: Block sweater. Thread ribbon through holes where front decrease starts. Tie in bow. On sleeves thread ribbon through holes to form a pleat. Tie a bow.

ALLERGY TO WOOL

I had been knitting since I was a young girl. Unfortunately, I found that I had a reaction to wool. So I began using cotton thread instead. I couldn't buy sweaters that weren't wool, so I knitted two matching sweaters of cotton, one for myself and one for Peggy, my six-year-old daughter. I had a little yarn left over so I knitted two more matching sweaters for Peggy's dolls. All were a medium blue color.

Windows Ground

Charted by Eugen Beugler.

Finished size: Repeat width 2 ½", repeat height 3".

Yarn: DMC Cebelia 10 (100% cotton; 260m/50g): white.

Needles: Size 2 (2.8 mm).

CO a multiple of 32 + 1 sts.

Row 1: *K6, k2tog, yo, k1, yo, ssk, k5, repeat from *, end last repeat k6.

Row 2 and all even rows: Purl.

Row 3: *K5, k2tog, yo, k3, yo, ssk, k4, repeat from *, end last repeat k5.

Row 5: *K3, k2tog, yo, k1, yo, ssk, yo, k3tog, yo, k1, yo, ssk, k2, repeat from *, end last repeat k3.

Row 7: *K2, k2tog, yo, k3, yo, sl 2tog k-wise, k1, p2sso, yo, k3, yo, ssk, k1, repeat from *, end last repeat k2.

Row 9: *K3, yo, ssk, yo, k3tog, yo, k1, yo, ssk, yo, k3tog, yo, k2, repeat from *, end last repeat k3.

Row 11: *K4, yo, sl 2tog k-wise, k1, p2sso, yo, k3, yo, sl 2tog k-wise, k1, p2sso, yo, k3, repeat from *, end last repeat k4.

Row 13: *K6, yo, ssk, yo, k3tog, yo, k5, repeat from *, end last repeat k6.

Row 15: *K7, yo, sl 2tog k-wise, k1, p2sso, yo, k6, repeat from *, end last repeat k7.

Row 17: *K1, yo, ssk, k11, k2tog, yo, repeat from *, end last repeat k2tog, yo, k1.

Row 19: *K2, yo, ssk, k9, k2tog, yo, k1, repeat from *, end last repeat k2.

Row 21: K1, k2tog, yo, k1, yo, ssk, k5, k2tog, yo, k1, yo, ssk, *yo, k3tog, yo, k1, yo, ssk, k5, k2tog, yo, k1, yo, ssk, repeat from *, end last repeat ssk, k1.

Row 23: K2tog, yo, k3, yo, ssk, k3, k2tog, yo, k3, yo, *sl 2tog k-wise, k1, p2sso, yo, k3, yo, ssk, k3, k2tog, yo, k3, yo, repeat from *, end last repeat k3, yo, ssk.

Row 25: *K1, yo, ssk, yo, k3tog, yo, k5, yo, ssk, yo, k3tog, yo, repeat from *, end last repeat k3tog, yo, k1.

Row 27: *K2, yo, sl 2tog k-wise, k1, p2sso, yo, k7, yo, sl 2tog k-wise, k1, p2sso, yo, k1, repeat from *, end last repeat k3tog, yo, k2.

Row 29: K1, k2tog, yo, k11, yo, ssk, *yo, k3tog, yo, k11, yo, ssk, repeat from *, end last repeat yo, ssk, k1.

Row 31: K2tog, yo, k13, yo, *sl 2tog k-wise, k1, p2sso, yo, k13, yo, repeat from *, end last repeat yo, k2tog.

Row 32: Purl.

Repeat Rows 1–32 for length desired.

Repeat from row 1 for length desired.

CO multiple of 32 + 1 sts.
All even rows: Purl.

Cable Stripe Ground

Finished size: Repeat width 2", repeat height ¾".

Yarn: DMC Cebelia 10 (100% cotton; 260m/50g): white.

Needles: Size 3 (3.2 mm), cable needle.

CO multiple of 12 sts. Knit 1 row.

Row 1: P1, k1, p2, k1, p1, (yo, ssk) 3 times.

Row 2 and all even rows: P6, k1, p1, k2, p1, k1.

Row 3: P1, k1, p2, k1, p1, (k2tog, yo) 3 times.

Row 5: P1, k1, p2, k1, p1, (yo, ssk) 3 times.

Row 7: P1, sl 3 sts onto cable needle and hold in back, k1. From cable needle, sl 2 sts back onto

Cable Stripe Ground.

left-hand needle and purl them. Sl third st back onto left-hand needle and knit it. P1, (k2tog, yo) 3 times.

Row 9: P1, k1, p2, k1, p1, (yo, ssk) 3 times.

Row 11: P1, k1, p2, k1, p1, (k2tog, yo) 3 times.

Row 13: P1, k1, p2, k1, p1, (yo, ssk) 3 times.

Row 15: P1, sl 3 sts to cable needle, hold in front, k1. From cable needle, sl 2 sts back onto left hand needle and purl them. Sl third st back onto left-hand needle and knit it. P1, (k2tog, yo) 3 times.

Row 16: P6, k1, p1, k2, p1, k1.

Repeat Rows 1–16 for length desired.

▣ **Row 7: sl 3 sts to cable needle, hold in back, k1. Sl 2 sts back to left-hand needle and purl them. Sl third st back to left-hand needle and knit it.**

Row 15: same except hold sts in front.

Even rows

CO multiple of 12 sts. Knit 1 row.

PRIZE-WINNING KNITTING

Meanwhile, I had noticed that *Woman's Day* magazine occasionally had patterns. In those days the magazine cost two cents, and even I could afford to keep track of it. When *Woman's Day* ran an article about prize-winning knitting (April 1943), I gladly paid the two cents for the issue. That was the start of my lifelong quest for patterns.

Mary 1935.

Fern Lace

Finished size: Depth 2 ¼", repeat interval 1".

Yarn: DMC Cebelia 30 (100% cotton; 515m/50g): color 992, 1 ball.

Needles: Size 0 (2.1mm).

Note: To CO at end of row: With fingers of left hand make a loop of thread, insert point of right-hand needle in loop; pull thread to tighten stitch.

CO 16 sts. Knit 1 row.

Row 1: Sl 1, k11, (yo, k2tog) 2 times, CO 1—17 sts.

Row 2 and all even rows: Knit.

Row 3: Sl 1, k10, (yo, k2tog)

⊡ **CO 1 st. With fingers of left hand make a loop of thread, insert point of right-hand needle in loop; pull thread to tighten stitch.**

CO 16 sts. Knit 1 row.
All even rows: Knit.

3 times, CO 1—18 sts.

Row 5: Sl 1, k9, (yo, k2tog) 4 times, CO 1—19 sts.

Row 7: Sl 1, k8, (yo, k2tog) 5 times, CO 1—20 sts.

Row 9: Sl 1, k7, (yo, k2tog) 6 times, CO 1—21 sts.

Row 11: Sl 1, k6, (yo, k2tog) 7 times, CO 1—22 sts.

Row 13: Sl 1, k5, (yo, k2tog) 8 times, CO 1—23 sts.

Row 15: Sl 1, k4, (yo, k2tog) 9 times, CO 1—24 sts.

Row 17: Sl 1, k3, (yo, k2tog) 10 times, CO 1—25 sts.

Row 19: Sl 1, k22, k2tog—24 sts.

Row 21: Sl 1, k3, (yo, k2tog) 10 times.

Row 23: Sl 1, k3, k2tog, (yo, k2tog) 9 times—23 sts.

Row 25: Sl 1, k4, k2tog, (yo, k2tog) 8 times—22 sts.

Row 27: Sl 1, k5, k2tog, (yo, k2tog) 7 times—21 sts.

Row 29: Sl 1, k6, k2tog, (yo, k2tog) 6 times—20 sts.

Row 31: Sl 1, k7, k2tog, (yo, k2tog) 5 times—19 sts.

Row 33: Sl 1, k8, k2tog, (yo, k2tog) 4 times—18 sts.

Row 35: Sl 1, k9, k2tog, (yo, k2tog) 3 times—17 sts.

Row 37: Sl 1, k10, k2tog, (yo, k2tog) 2 times—16 sts.

Row 39: Sl 1, k11, k2tog, yo, k2tog, CO 1.

Row 40: Knit.

Repeat Rows 1–40 for length desired.

From left to right: Double Diamond Edging, Aunt Jennie's Shark's Tooth Edging, and Fern Lace.

FLOWER IN THE TREETOP

One day my husband Rene, daughter Peggy, and I went for a walk in the Brooklyn Botanic Garden. Peggy got tired so she and I rested while Rene went on walking. He brought back a twig from a "tulip" tree (*Liriodendron tulipifera*) which had a flower on the end. I looked at it and decided to knit it as a doily for my sofa. I was doing ovals that year. This is the pattern I came up with.

Flower-in-the-Treetop Doily

Finished size: Approximately 13" × 18".

Yarn: DMC Cebelia 10 (100% cotton; 260m/50g): white, 1 ball.

Needles: Size 2 (2.8 mm): set of five dpn, 21" circular.

Notions: Size F crochet hook, markers.

CO 2 sts on each of 3 dpn. On Rounds 1 through 30, repeat each instruction 6 times unless otherwise instructed. When there is a double yo in the previous round, k and p in the double yo.

Rnd 1: Knit—6 sts total.

Rnd 2: K in front and back of each st—12 sts.

Rnd 3 and all odd rnds: Knit.

Rnd 4: K in front and back of st, k1—18 sts.

Rnd 6: K in front and back of each st—36 sts.

Rnd 8: K1, yo, ssk, yo, k1, yo, k2tog, yo—48 sts.

Rnd 10: K1, yo, ssk, (k1, yo) twice, k1, k2tog, yo—60 sts.

Rnd 12: K1, yo, ssk, k2, yo, k1, yo, k2, k2tog, yo—72 sts.

Rnd 14: K1, yo, ssk, k3, yo, k1, yo, k3, k2tog, yo—84 sts.

Rnd 16: K1, yo, ssk, k4, yo, k1, yo, k4, k2tog, yo—96 sts.

Rnd 18: K1, yo, ssk, k5, yo, k1, yo, k5, k2tog, yo—108 sts.

Rnd 20: (K1, yo) twice, ssk, k4, yo, k3, yo, k4, k2tog, yo, k1, yo—132 sts.

Rnd 22: (K1, yo, ssk) twice, k4, yo, sl 2tog k-wise, k1, p2sso, yo, k4, k2tog, yo, k1, k2tog, yo—132 sts.

Rnd 24: K1, yo, k2tog, yo twice, ssk, yo, ssk, k9, k2tog, yo, k2tog, yo twice, ssk, yo—144 sts.

Rnd 26: Yo, k1, yo twice, sl 2tog k-wise, k1, p2sso twice, yo twice, ssk, k7, k2tog, yo twice, sl 2tog k-wise, k1, p2sso twice, yo—132 sts.

Rnd 28: K3, yo, k2tog, yo twice, ssk, k1, yo, ssk, k5, k2tog, yo, k1, k2tog, yo twice, ssk, yo—144 sts.

Rnd 30: Yo, sl 2tog k-wise, k1, p2sso, yo, k1, yo twice, ssk, (k2tog, yo twice, ssk) twice, k1, yo twice, (ssk, k2tog, yo twice) 2 times, k1—162 sts.

Rnd 31: Add fourth needle and work as follows. Needle 1: k 28, k2tog. Needle 2: k 51. Needle 3: k28 k2tog. Needle 4: k51.

Slip 12 sts onto each end of needles 1 and 3, making 59 sts, leaving 48 sts on needles 2 and 4. Knit needles 1 and 2. On needle 3:

1st and 3rd needles	2nd and 4th needles
Rnd 32: Yo, sl 2tog k-wise, k1, p2sso, yo, k2, (k2tog, yo twice, ssk) 2 times, k1, k2tog, k1, (k2tog, yo twice, ssk) 2 times, k2, and from next needle, yo, k2 tog, yo—29 sts.	K2, (k2tog, yo twice, ssk) 5 times, k7, (k2tog, yo twice, ssk) 5 times, k2—51 sts.
Rnd 34: Yo, k3, yo, (k2tog, yo twice, ssk) 2 times, k2tog, yo, sl 2tog k-wise, k1, p2sso, yo, ssk, (k2tog, yo twice, ssk) 2 times, yo, k3, yo—31 sts.	(K2tog, yo twice, ssk) 5 times, k5, inc 2, k5, (k2tog, yo twice, ssk) 5 times—53 sts.
Rnd 36: Yo, k5, yo, k2, (k2tog, yo twice, ssk) 2 times, yo, k1, yo, (k2tog, yo twice, ssk) 2 times, k2, yo, k5, yo—37 sts.	K2, (k2tog, yo twice, ssk) 4 times, k8, inc 2, k8, (k2tog, yo twice, ssk) 4 times, k2—55 sts.
Rnd 38: Yo, k7, yo, (k2tog, yo twice, ssk) 2 times, k2tog, yo, sl 2tog k-wise, k1, p2sso, yo, ssk, (k2tog, yo twice, ssk) 2 times, yo, k7, yo—39 sts.	(K2tog, yo twice, ssk) 4 times, k11, inc 2, k11, (k2tog, yo twice, ssk) 4 times—57 sts.
Rnd 40: K3, sl 2tog k-wise, k1, p2sso, k3, yo, k2, (k2tog, yo twice, ssk) 2 times, yo, k1, yo, (k2tog, yo twice, ssk) 2 times, yo, k3, sl 2tog k-wise, k1, p2sso, k3—39 sts.	Yo, k2, (k2tog, yo twice, ssk) 4 times, k10, inc 2, k10, (k2tog, yo twice, ssk) 4 times, k2, yo—61 sts.
Rnd 42: K2, sl 2tog k-wise, k1, p2sso, k2, yo, sl 2tog k-wise, k1, p2sso, yo twice, ssk, k2tog, yo twice, ssk, k2tog, yo, sl 2tog k-wise, k1, p2sso, yo, ssk, k2tog, yo twice, ssk, k2tog, yo twice, sl 2tog k-wise, k1, p2sso, yo twice, k2, sl 2tog k-wise, k1, p2sso, k2—34 sts.	Yo, k3tog, yo twice, ssk, (k2tog, yo twice, ssk) 5 times, k5, inc 2, k5, (k2tog, yo twice, ssk) 5 times, k2tog, yo twice, k3tog, yo—63 sts.

Go to Charts 2 and 3 for Row 31 and beyond.

```
(162) | I O O / \ O O / \ O O I \ O O / \ O O / \ O O I O ∧ O | 30
(144)   | O \ O O / I O / I I I I I I \ O I \ O O / O I I |     28
(132)   | O ∧ ∧ O O / I I I I I I I I \ O O ∧ ∧ O O I O |       26
(144)  | O \ O O / O / I I I I I I I I \ O \ O O / O I |        24
(132)   | O / I O / I I I I O ∧ O I I I I \ O I \ O I |         22
(132)   | O I O / I I I I I O I I I O I I I I \ O I O I |       20
(108)    | O / I I I I I O I I I \ O I |                        18
 (96)     | O / I I I I I O I O I I I I \ O I |                 16
 (84)      | O / I I I O I O I I I \ O I |                      14
 (72)       | O / I I O I O I I \ O I |                         12
 (60)        | O / I O I O I \ O I |                            10
 (48)         | O / O I O \ O I |                               8
 (36)          | M M M |                                       6
 (18)           | I M |                                        4
 (12)            | M |                                         2
  (6)             | I |                                        1
```

Numbers in ( ) at left of chart are total st counts.
CO 6 sts on 3 needles. Odd rnds are knit.
Repeat Chart 1 six times.

Chart 1

1st and 3rd needles	2nd and 4th needles

1st and 3rd needles

Rnd 44: K1, sl 2tog k-wise, k1, p2sso, k1, yo, k3, k2tog, yo twice, ssk, k9, k2tog, yo twice, ssk, k3, yo, ssk, k1, sl 2tog k-wise, k1, p2sso, k1—31 sts.

Rnd 46: Sl 2tog k-wise, k1, p2sso, yo, k2, k2tog, yo twice, ssk, k6, inc 2, k6, k2tog, yo twice, ssk, k2, yo, sl 2tog k-wise, k1, p2sso—31 sts.

Rnd 48: K2, k2tog, yo twice, ssk, k9, inc 2, k9, k2tog, yo twice, ssk, k2—33 sts.

Rnd 50: K2tog, yo twice, ssk, k12, inc 2, k12, k2tog, yo twice, ssk—35 sts.

2nd and 4th needles

Yo, k3, (k2tog, yo twice, ssk) 5 times, k8, inc 2, k8, (k2tog, yo twice, ssk) 5 times, k3, yo—67 sts.

Yo, k2, (k2tog, yo twice, ssk) 6 times, k7, inc 2, k7, (k2tog, yo twice, ssk) 6 times, k2, yo—71 sts.

K1, (k2tog, yo twice, ssk) 8 times, k3tog, yo twice, ssk, (k2tog, yo twice, ssk) 8 times, k1—70 sts.

K1, yo twice, ssk, (k2tog, yo twice, ssk) 16 times, k2tog, yo twice, k1—72 sts.

Rnd 52: K2, (k2tog, yo twice, ssk) 3 times, k15, inc 2, k15, (k2tog, yo twice, ssk) 3 times, k2—61 sts.

Rnd 53: Sl 1, p58, turn.

Rnd 54: Sl 1, k1, (k2tog, yo twice, ssk) 2 times, k18, inc 2, k18, (k2tog, yo twice, ssk) 2 times, k2—59 sts.

Rnd 55: Sl 1, p56, turn.

Rnd 56: Sl 1, k1, (k2tog, yo twice, ssk) 2 times, k17, inc 2, k17, (k2tog, yo twice, ssk) 2 times, k2—57 sts, turn.

Rnd 57: Sl 1, p54, turn.

Rnd 58: Sl 1, k1, (k2tog, yo twice, ssk) 2 times, k16, inc 2, k16,

Go to Chart 4.

Add fourth needle. Knit Row 31 as indicated.

Chart 2—Needles 1 and 3.

(k2tog, yo twice, ssk) 2 times, k2—55 sts, turn.

Rnd 59: Sl 1, p52, turn.

Rnd 60: Sl 1, k1, (k2tog, yo twice, ssk) 3 times, k11, inc 2, k11, (k2tog, yo twice, ssk) 3 times, k2—53 sts, turn.

Rnd 61: Sl 1, p50, turn.

Rnd 62: Sl 1, k1, (k2tog, yo twice, ssk) 2 times, k14, inc 2, k14, (k2tog, yo twice, ssk) 2 times, k2—51 sts, turn.

Rnd 63: Sl 1, p48, turn.

Rnd 64: Sl 1, k1, (k2tog, yo twice, ssk) 2 times, k13, inc 2, k13, (k2tog, yo twice, ssk) 2 times, k2—49 sts, turn.

Rnd 65: Sl 1, p46, turn.

Rnd 66: Sl 1, k1, (k2tog, yo twice, ssk) 3 times, k8, inc 2, k8, (k2tog, yo twice, ssk) 3 times, k2—47 sts, turn.

Rnd 67: Sl 1, p44, turn.

Rnd 68: Sl 1, k1, (k2tog, yo twice, ssk) 2 times, k11, inc 2, k11, (k2tog, yo twice, ssk) 2 times, k2, turn.

Rnd 69: Sl 1, p42, turn.

Rnd 70: Sl 1, k1, (k2tog, yo twice, ssk) 2 times, k10, inc 2, k10, (k2tog, yo twice, ssk) 2 times, k2—43 sts, turn.

Rnd 71: Sl 1, p40, turn.

Rnd 72: Sl 1, k1, (k2tog, yo twice, ssk) 4 times, k1, yo twice, ssk, (k2tog, yo twice, ssk) 4 times, k2—40 sts, turn.

Rnd 73: Sl 1, p37, turn.

Rnd 74: Sl 1, k1, (k2tog, yo twice, ssk) 8 times, k24—58 sts.

Knit the 4th needle. Repeat rnds 52 to 74 on needle 1.

Go to Chart 5 after knitting chart 4 on needles 1 and 3.

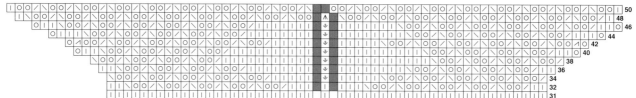

Knit row 31 as indicated.

Chart 3—Needles 2 and 4.

Go to Chart 5.

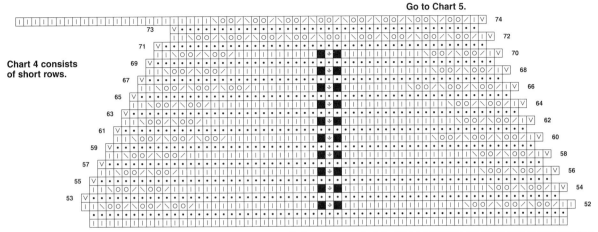

Chart 4 consists of short rows.

Knit across needle 3 first then, following the chart, knit across needle 1.

Chart 4

See written instruction for crochet finishing.

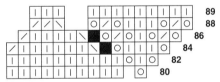

Change to circular needle, mark 1st round.
Rounds 75–78 knit. Round 79 adjust to 240 sts.
Repeat Chart 5 24 times.

Chart 5

Rnd 75: Knit onto circular needle marking the beginning of the rnd—260 sts.

Rnd 76: Knit.

Rnd 77: Knit.

Rnd 78: Knit.

Rnd 79: Knit and count sts, adjust to 240 sts.

Rnds 80 through 89: Repeat 24 times.

Rnd 80: Yo, k10—264 sts.

Rnd 82: Yo, k1, yo, k10—312 sts.

Rnd 84: Yo, k3, yo, ssk, k6, k2tog— 312 sts.

Rnd 86: Yo, k2tog, yo, k1, yo, k2tog, yo, ssk, k4, k2tog—312 sts.

Rnd 88: Yo, k2tog, yo, k3, yo, k2tog, yo, ssk, k2tog twice—264 sts.

Rnd 89: Knit.

Finishing: With the crochet hook, pick up 3 sts and sc through them, ch 8, repeat around. Block into an ellipse.

BROOKLYN LIBRARY

I learned that the Brooklyn Public Library had a very good collection of knitting books, from which I copied patterns to add to my collection. I would take the bus and go to the Botanic Garden first. Then I would walk over to the library to get books and take the bus back. The newspaper ran an editorial saying there were too many buses. I wrote the paper and said there weren't too many buses when you had to wait for three buses before one would stop to pick you up.

Open Zigzag Ground

Finished size: Repeat width 1 ½", repeat height 1 ½".
Yarn: DMC Cebelia 10 (100% cotton; 260m/50g): ecru.
Needles: Size 1 (2.4 mm).

CO a multiple of 22 + 4 sts. Knit 1 row.

Row 1: K1, yo, ssk, k1, yo, k1, k2tog, yo, ssk, k3, *yo, ssk, k1, yo, k1, k2tog, yo, ssk, k3, repeat from *, end k6.

Row 2 and all even rows: Purl.

Row 3: K2, yo, ssk, k1, k2tog, yo, k1, yo, ssk, k2, *k1, yo, ssk, k1, k2tog, yo, k1, yo, ssk, k2, repeat from *, end k5.

Row 5: K3, yo, k3tog, yo, k3, yo, ssk, k1, *k2, yo, sl 2tog k-wise, k1, p2sso, yo, k3, yo, ssk, k1, repeat from *, end k4.

Row 7: K4, yo, ssk, k1, yo, k1, k2tog, yo, ssk, *k3, yo, ssk, k1, yo, k1, k2tog, yo, ssk, repeat from *, end k3.

Row 9: K5, yo, ssk, k1, k2tog, yo, k1, yo, *ssk, k3, yo, ssk, k1, k2tog, yo, k1, yo, repeat from *, end ssk, k2.

Row 11: K6, yo, sl 2tog k-wise, k1, p2sso, yo, k3, *yo, ssk, k3, yo, sl 2tog k-wise, k1, p2sso, yo, k3, repeat from *, end yo, ssk, k1.

Row 13: K6, k2tog, yo, ssk, k1, yo, k1, *k2tog, yo, k3, k2tog, yo, ssk,

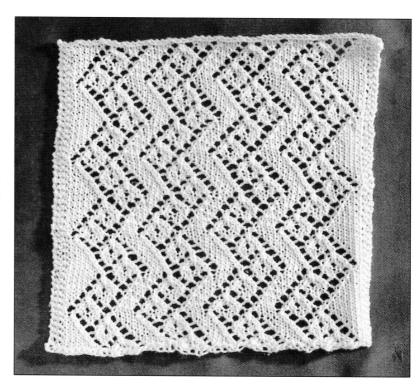

End └──── **Repeat** ────┘

CO multiple of 22 + 4 sts. Knit 1 row.
Purl all even rows.

k1, yo, k1, repeat from *, end k2tog, yo, k1.

Row 15: K5, k2tog, yo, k1, yo, ssk, k1, k2tog, *yo, k3, k2tog, yo, k1, yo, ssk, k1, k2tog, repeat from *, end yo, k2.

Row 17: K4, k2tog, yo, k3, yo, sl 2tog k-wise, k1, p2sso, yo, *k3, k2tog, yo, k3, yo, sl 2tog k-wise, k1, p2sso, yo, repeat from * end k3.

Row 19: K3, k2tog, yo, ssk, k1, yo, k1, k2tog, yo, k1, *k2, k2tog, yo, ssk, k1, yo, k1, k2tog, yo, k1, repeat from *, end k4.

Row 21: K2, k2tog, yo, k1, yo, ssk, k1, k2tog, yo, k2, *k1, k2tog, yo, k1, yo, ssk, k1, k2tog, yo, k2, repeat from *, end k5.

Row 23: K1, k2tog, yo, k3, yo, sl 2tog k-wise, k1, p2sso, yo, k3, *k2tog, yo, k3, yo, sl 2tog k-wise, k1, p2sso, yo, k3, repeat from *, end k6.

Row 24: Purl.

PLASTIC DOILIES

My most exotic source of patterns was two plastic doilies I picked up in a store near where I changed buses. They cost fifteen cents each. They felt like raw liver, but they were pressed from the knitted lace originals clearly enough so that I could write the directions. These two doilies and a Japanese Christmas card were all I ever bought in that store.

"Plastic" Doily

Charted by Dr. Rowena Spencer from Mary Schiffmann's pattern.

Finished size: 18" diameter.
Yarn: DMC Cebelia 20, (100% cotton; 370 m/50 g): ecru, 2 balls.

Needles: Size 0 (2.1 mm): set of 4 10" dpn, size 0 (2.1 mm): 16" and 24" circular needles.

Notions: Size 5 crochet hook.

CO 8 sts on 4 needles. When the number of sts has increased significantly, change to a circular needle and later change again to a larger circular needle. Instructions are for the number of repeats indicated. All odd-numbered rounds are knit *except Rounds 99 and 101*.

8 repeats.
Rnd 1: Knit—1 st.
Rnd 2: Yo, k1—2 sts.
Rnd 4: Yo, k2—3 sts.
Rnd 6: Yo, k3—4 sts.
Rnd 8: Yo, k4—5 sts.
Rnd 10: Yo, k5—6 sts.
Rnd 12: Yo, k1, yo, ssk, k3—7 sts.
Rnd 14: Yo, k3, yo, ssk, k2—8 sts.

Rnd 16: Yo, k1, yo, sl 2tog k-wise, k1, p2sso, yo, k1, yo, ssk, k1—9 sts.
Rnd 18: Yo, k3, yo, k1, yo, k3, yo, ssk—12 sts.
Rnd 20: K1, yo, sl 2tog k-wise, k1, p2sso, yo, k3, yo, sl 2tog k-wise, k1, p2sso, yo, k2.
Rnd 22: K—96 sts total.
Rnd 24: *Yo, k2tog, rep from *.
Rnd 26: *Yo, k2tog, rep from *.
Rnd 28: *Yo, k2tog, rep from *.
Rnd 30: *Yo, k2tog, rep from *.
Rnd 32: Knit.

24 repeats.
Rnd 34: K2tog, yo, ssk, yo—4 sts.
Rnd 36: K1, yo, k1, ssk, yo—5 sts.
Rnd 38: K1, yo, k2, ssk, yo—6 sts.
Rnd 40: K1, yo, k3, ssk, yo—7 sts.
Rnd 42: K1, yo, k4, ssk, yo—8 sts.

Rnd 44: K1, yo, k5, ssk, yo—9 sts.
Rnd 46: K1, yo, k1, k2tog, k3, ssk, yo.
Slip 1 st to the left.
Rnd 48: Yo, k3, sl 2tog k-wise, k1, p2sso, k3—8 sts.
Rnd 50: Yo, k1, yo, k2, sl 2tog k-wise, k1, p2sso, k2.
Rnd 52: Yo, k3, yo, k1, sl 2tog k-wise, k1, p2sso, k1.

48 repeats.
Rnd 54: Yo, k1, yo, sl 2tog k-wise, k1, p2sso—4 sts.
Rnd 56: Yo, k3, yo, k1—6 sts.
Slip 1 st to the right.
Rnd 58: Yo, sl 2tog k-wise, k1, p2sso, yo, k3—6 sts.
Rnd 60: Yo, k3, yo, sl 2tog k-wise, k1, p2sso.
Slip 1 st to the right.

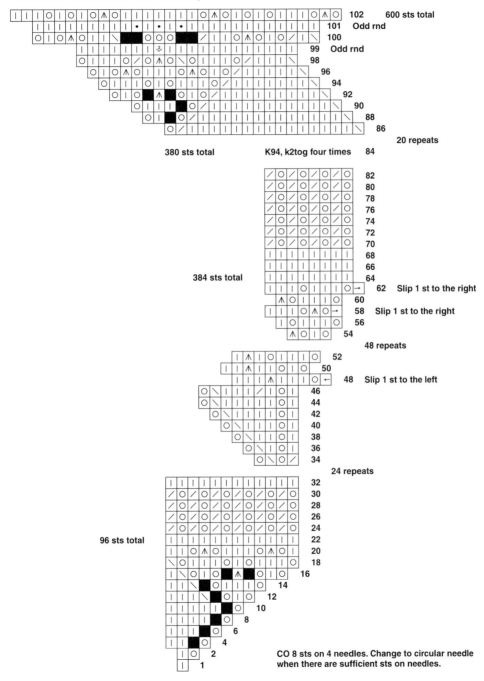

See written instruction for crochet finishing.

102 600 sts total
101 Odd rnd
100
99 Odd rnd
98
96
94
92
90
88
86
20 repeats
380 sts total
K94, k2tog four times 84

82
80
78
76
74
72
70
68
66
384 sts total 64
62 Slip 1 st to the right
60
58 Slip 1 st to the right
56
54
48 repeats

52
50
48 Slip 1 st to the left
46
44
42
40
38
36
34
24 repeats

32
30
28
26
24
22
96 sts total 20
18
16
14
12
10
8
6
4
2
1

CO 8 sts on 4 needles. Change to circular needle
when there are sufficient sts on needles.

Rnd 62: Yo, k3, yo, k3—8 sts.

Rnd 64: Knit—384 sts total.

Rnd 66: Knit.

Rnd 68: Knit.

Rnd 70: Yo, k2tog.

Rnd 72: Yo, k2tog.

Rnd 74: Yo, k2tog.

Rnd 76: Yo, k2tog.

Rnd 78: Yo, k2tog.

Rnd 80: Yo, k2tog.

Rnd 82: Yo, k2tog.

Rnd 84: (K94, k2tog) 4 times—380 sts total.

20 repeats.

Rnd 86: Ssk, k15, k2tog, yo—18 sts.

Rnd 88: Ssk, k13, k2tog, yo, k1, yo.

Rnd 90: Ssk, k11, k2tog, yo, k3, yo.

Rnd 92: Ssk, k9, k2tog, yo, k1, yo, sl 2tog k-wise, k1, p2sso, yo, k1, yo.

Rnd 94: Ssk, k7, k2tog, yo, k3, yo, k1, yo, k3, yo—20 sts.

Rnd 96: Ssk, k5, k2tog, yo, k1, yo, sl 2tog k-wise, k1, p2sso, yo, k3, yo, sl 2tog k-wise, k1, p2sso, yo, k1, yo.

Rnd 98: Ssk, k3, k2tog, yo, k3, yo, ssk, yo, sl 2tog k-wise, k1, p2sso, yo, k2tog, yo, k3, yo.

Rnd 99: K12, k1, p1 in same st, k7—21 sts.

Rnd 100: Ssk, k1, k2tog, yo, k1, yo, sl 2tog k-wise, k1, p2sso, yo, k2, k2tog, yo 3 times, ssk, k2, yo, sl 2tog k-wise, k1, p2sso, yo, k1, yo—22 sts.

Rnd 101: K11, (k1, p1, k1, p1, k1, p1, k1) in the "yo 3 times", k8—26 sts.

Rnd 102: Yo, sl 2tog k-wise, k1, p2sso, yo, k3, (yo, k1) twice, yo, sl 2tog k-wise, k1, p2sso, yo, k7, yo, sl 2tog k-wise, k1, p2sso, (yo, k1) twice, yo, k3—30 sts.

Rnd 103: Knit—600 sts total.

Crochet off. Sc in 3 sts, ch 7 between.

A VISIT TO CORNWALLIS'S HEADQUARTERS

One day in 1948, my husband, daughter, and I took a picnic lunch on a hike along the New Jersey shore of the Hudson River. We stopped at the headquarters of Charles Cornwallis, a British general during the Revolutionary War. There, on a bed in one of the rooms, an historical society had placed a bedspread of unbleached muslin with an edging of knitted lace. There was glass across the doorway so you could only look in but, fortunately, the knitting was done in heavy thread. I took notes on the lace pattern, writing on the heading of the *New York Times*, which I was carrying. The edging was made in three parts: one was a standard pattern, one was like a pattern I already had, and the third was fairly simple. That night, after I put my family to bed, I stayed up and wrote out the directions.

Cornwallis Lace

Finished size: Depth 3 ½", repeat interval 2".

Yarn: DMC Cordonnet 30 (100% cotton; 197m/20g): white.

Needles: Size 1 (2.4 mm).

CO 27 sts. Knit 1 row.

Row 1: Sl 1, k2, (yo, k2tog) 2 times, k1, yo, k2tog, k5, yo, k2tog, k3, yo twice, k2tog, k5—28 sts.

Row 2 and all even rows, except

rows 14 and 28: Knit, except k1, p1 in "yo twice".

Row 3: Sl 1, k2, (yo, k2tog) 2 times, k2, yo, k2tog, k5, yo, k2tog, k10.

Row 5: Sl 1, k2, (yo, k2tog) 2 times, k1, (yo, k2tog) 2 times, k3, yo, k2tog, k3, (yo twice, k2tog) 2 times, k4—30 sts.

Row 7: Sl 1, k2, (yo, k2tog) 2 times, k2, (yo, k2tog) 2 times, k3, yo, k2tog, k12.

Row 9: Sl 1, k2, (yo, k2tog) 2 times, k1, (yo, k2tog) 3 times, k1, yo, k2tog, k3, (yo twice, k2tog) 3 times, k4—33 sts.

Row 11: Sl 1, k2, (yo, k2tog) 2 times, k2, (yo, k2tog) 2 times, k3, yo, k2tog, k15.

Row 13: Sl 1, k2, (yo, k2tog) 2 times, k3, (yo, k2tog) 2 times, k1, yo, k2tog, k16.

Row 14: BO 6, k26—27 sts.

Row 15: Sl 1, k2, (yo, k2tog) 2 times, k4, yo, k2tog, k3, yo, k2tog, k2, yo twice, k2tog, k5—28 sts.

Row 17: Sl 1, k2, (yo, k2tog) 2 times, k5, yo, k2tog, k1, yo, k2tog, k11.

Row 19: Sl 1, k2, (yo, k2tog) 2 times, k9, yo, k2tog, k2, (yo twice, k2tog) 2 times, k4—30 sts.

Row 21: Sl 1, k2, (yo, k2tog)

2 times, k8, yo, k2tog, k13.

Row 23: Sl 1, k2, (yo, k2tog) 2 times, k9, yo, k2tog, k2, (yo twice, k2tog) 3 times, k4—33 sts.

Row 25: Sl 1, k2, (yo, k2tog) 2 times, k8, yo, k2tog, k16.

Row 27: Sl 1, k2, (yo, k2tog) 2 times, k9, yo, k2tog, k15.

Row 28: BO 6, k26—27 sts.

Repeat Rows 1–28 for length desired.

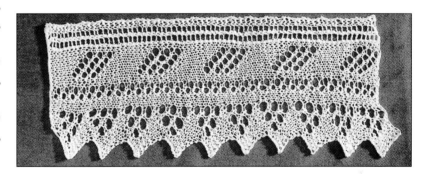

Repeat from Row 1 for length desired.

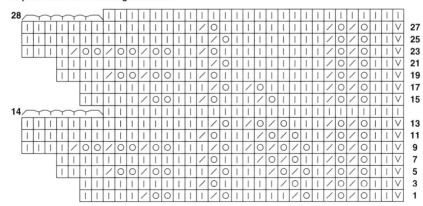

CO 27 sts. Knit 1 row.

THE COOPER UNION MUSEUM

In 1956, I phoned the Cooper Union Museum in New York City and asked to see their knitted laces. They had two samplers, one with twenty-four patterns and another with thirty patterns. The samplers were similar to American-made embroidery samplers. I took notes on two or three patterns at a time, then went home and wrote them out. When I finished those, I'd go back for more. I knitted each pattern up twice, once for me and once for the museum. Later, I knitted up some of the patterns to make a sampler ten patterns long for my sister-in-law. I also made one twelve patterns long for me which I hung in my stairway.

Today the Cooper Union Museum is known as the Cooper-Hewitt National Design Museum and is part of the Smithsonian Institute.

Star Doily

This is the pattern I use to teach knitting in the round and it contains several tips for beginning lace knitters.

Finished size: 12" diameter.
Yarn: DMC Cebelia 10 (100% cotton; 260m/50g): white, 1 ball.

Needles: Size 2 (2.8 mm): set of 5 dpn, 16" circular needle.
Notions: Size 5 crochet hook, 8 markers.

CO 8 sts on 4 needles (2 sts on each needle). Join, being careful not to twist sts.

Repeat each pattern 8 times.

Mary's Teaching Notes

Place a marker for beg of rnd; slip marker on each following rnd.

Rnd 1 and all odd numbered rnds: Knit.

Rnd 2: Yo, k1—2 sts.

Mary's Teaching Notes

Throughout the pattern, each yo counts as 1 stitch.

Rnd 4: (Yo, k1) 2 times—4 sts.

Rnd 6: Yo, k3, yo, k1—6 sts.

Rnd 8: Yo, ssk, k1, k2tog, yo, k1.

Rnd 10: Yo, k1, yo, sl 2tog k-wise, k1, p2sso, (yo, k1) 2 times—8 sts.

Rnd 12: (Yo, k3, yo, k1) 2 times—12 sts, 96 sts total.

Rnd 14: (Yo, ssk, k1, k2tog, yo, k1) 2 times.

Rnd 16: (K1, yo, sl 2tog k-wise, k1, p2sso, yo, k2) 2 times.

Rnd 18: Yo, ssk, k1, yo, ssk, k1, k2tog, yo, k1, k2tog, yo, k1.

Rnd 20: K1, yo, ssk, k1, yo, sl 2tog k-wise, k1, p2sso, yo, k1, k2tog, yo, k2.

Rnd 22: K2, yo, ssk, k3, k2tog, yo, k3.

Rnd 24: K3, yo, ssk, k1, k2tog, yo, k4.

Rnd 26: K4, yo, sl 2tog k-wise, k1, p2sso, yo, k4, yo, k1, yo—14 sts, 112 sts total.

Mary's Teaching Notes

Change to 16" circular needle.

Rnd 28: Ssk, k3, yo, k1, yo, k3, k2tog, yo, k3, yo—16 sts, 128 sts total.

Rnd 30: Ssk, k7, k2tog, yo, k1, yo, sl 2tog k-wise, k1, p2sso, yo, k1, yo.

Rnd 32: Ssk, k5, k2tog, yo, k3, yo, k1, yo, k3, yo—18 sts, 144 sts total.

See written instruction for crochet finishing.

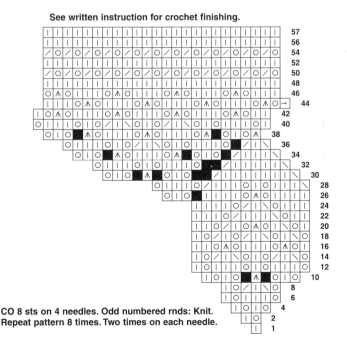

**CO 8 sts on 4 needles. Odd numbered rnds: Knit.
Repeat pattern 8 times. Two times on each needle.**

Rnd 34: Ssk, k3, k2tog, yo, k1, yo, sl 2tog k-wise, k1, p2sso, yo, k3, yo, sl 2tog k-wise, k1, p2sso, yo, k1, yo.

Rnd 36: Ssk, k1, k2tog, yo, k3, yo, k1, yo, ssk, k1, k2tog, yo, k1, yo, k3, yo—20 sts, 160 sts total.

Rnd 38: Sl 2tog k-wise, k1, p2sso, yo, k1, yo, (sl 2tog k-wise, k1, p2sso, yo, k3, yo) 2 times, sl 2tog k-wise, k1, p2sso, yo, k1, yo.

Rnd 40: K1, yo, k3, yo, k1, yo, ssk, k1, k2tog, yo, k1, yo, ssk, k1, k2tog, yo, k1, yo, k3, yo—24 sts, 192 sts total.

Rnd 42: K2, yo, sl 2tog k-wise, k1, p2sso, (yo, k3, yo, sl 2tog k-wise, k1, p2sso) 3 times, yo, k1.

Mary's Teaching Notes

Sl last st to right needle unworked. Remove marker for beg of rnd; sl last st back to left needle. Replace marker for beg of rnd.

Rnd 44: Yo, sl 2tog k-wise, k1,

p2sso, yo, k3, repeat around.

Rnd 46: K3, yo, sl 2tog k-wise, k1, p2sso, yo, repeat around.

Rnd 48: Knit.

Rnd 50: Yo, k2tog, repeat around.

Rnd 52: Knit.

Rnd 54: Yo, k2tog, repeat around.

Rnd 56: Knit.

Rnd 57: Knit.

Mary's Teaching Notes
Bind off Doily with Crochet

Doilies are often bound off with a crochet chain edge. With crochet hook, draw up a loop in first st, leaving st on needle. *Ch 8, (insert hook in next st and sl st off needle) 3 times (4 loops now on hook), yo hook and draw through all 4 loops on hook, rep from * around. Join with a sl st in beg ch; finish off.

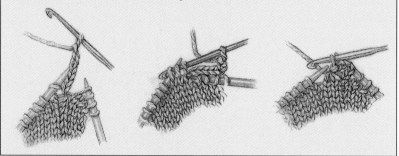

Bind off doily with crochet as described above.

Finishing: Weave in all ends. Place on a flat padded surface. Pin outer edge using rust-proof pins. Spray with commercial spray starch until wet. Let dry thoroughly before removing pins.

Ribbed Stripe Ground

Finished size: Repeat width 2", repeat height ½".

Yarn: DMC Cebelia 10 (100% cotton; 260m/50g): white, 1 ball.

Needles: Size 2 (2.8 mm).

CO multiple of 16 sts.

Notes: The sample shows three repeats across with one edge stitch on each side.

CO multiple of 16 sts.
Row 1: Yo, ssk, k3, k2tog, yo, (k1, p1) 4 times, k1.
Row 2: (P1, k1) 4 times, p8.
Row 3: K1, yo, ssk, k1, k2tog, yo, k2, (P1, k1) 4 times.
Row 4: (P1, k1) 4 times, p3, yo, p3tog, yo, p2.

THE STORY OF AMERICAN NEEDLEWORK

*W*oman's Day magazine contacted the Cooper Union Museum in connection with a series of articles being prepared by Rose Wilder Lane titled "The Story of American Needlework". One article was to be on knitted lace. Cooper Union recommended that *Woman's Day* ask me to write out patterns. I wrote directions for pieces that Rose sent me, such as a christening dress and Bernadin's sampler now in the Laura Ingalls Wilder Museum, Mansfield, Missouri (Rose was Laura's daughter). Rose arranged for pieces from other museums such as the Stamford Historical Society, Stamford, Connecticut, Newark Museum, Newark, New Jersey, and Witte Museum, San Antonio, Texas, to be sent to the editorial offices of *Woman's Day* where I was working on contract.

The article on knitted lace appeared in the October, 1961 issue of *Woman's Day*. My printed directions for the pictured laces were offered to knitters who sent in fifty cents. However, my name did not appear in the article.

Christening Dress

Four different laces are used for this christening dress made for a three-month-old baby: two insertions and two edgings. Two balls of DMC Cebelia 30 is sufficient to knit all the insertions and edgings. You may incorporate the lace into a dress made from your own or a commercially-available pattern, or you could add the lace to an existing garment.

Christening Dress—Narrow Edging

Narrow edging is used around the sleeves.

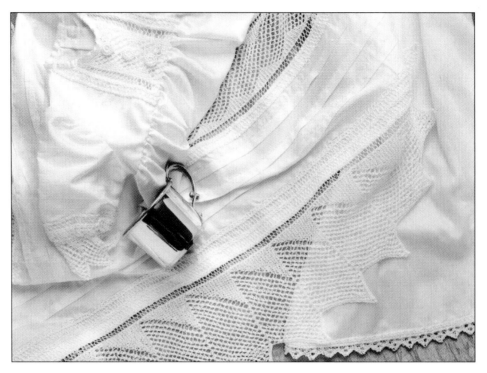

Christening Dress.

Finished size: Depth 3", repeat interval 1 ¼".

Yarn: DMC Cebelia 30 (100% cotton; 515m/50g): white.

Needles: Size 1 (2.4 mm).

Notions: Size 22 tapestry needle.

CO 21 sts. Knit 1 row.

Row 1: Sl 1, k2, yo, k2tog, k2, yo, k2tog, k1, (yo, k2tog) 5 times, yo, k1—22 sts.

Row 2: K15, yo, k2tog, k2, yo, k2tog, k1.

Row 3: Sl 1, k2, (yo, k2tog, k2) 2 times, (yo, k2tog) 5 times, yo, k1—23 sts.

Repeat from Row 1 for length desired.

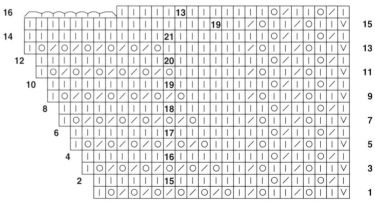

CO 21 sts. Knit 1 row.

Narrow Edging

Row 4: K16, yo, k2tog, k2, yo, k2tog, k1.

Row 5: Sl 1, k2, yo, k2tog, k2, yo, k2tog, k3, (yo, k2tog) 5 times, yo, k1—24 sts.

Row 6: K17, yo, k2tog, k2, yo, k2tog, k1.

Row 7: Sl 1, k2, yo, k2tog, k2, yo, k2tog, k4, (yo, k2tog) 5 times, yo, k1—25 sts.

Row 8: K18, yo, k2tog, k2, yo, k2tog, k1.

Row 9: Sl 1, k2, yo, k2tog, k2, yo, k2tog, k5, (yo, k2tog) 5 times, yo, k1—26 sts.

Row 10: K19, yo, k2tog, k2, yo, k2tog, k1.

Row 11: Sl 1, k2, yo, k2tog, k2, yo, k2tog, k6, (yo, k2tog) 5 times, yo, k1—27 sts.

Row 12: K20, yo, k2tog, k2, yo, k2tog, k1.

Row 13: Sl 1, k2, yo, k2tog, k2, yo, k2tog, k7, (yo, k2tog) 5 times, yo, k1—28 sts.

Row 14: K21, yo, k2tog, k2, yo, k2tog, k1.

Row 15: Sl 1, (k2, yo, k2tog) 2 times, k19.

Row 16: BO 7, k13, yo, k2tog, k2, yo, k2tog, k1—21 sts.

Repeat Rows 1–16 for 6 repeats total.

Finishing: Graft beginning and ending edges together.

Christening Dress— Wide Edging

Wide Edging is used around the bottom of the skirt.

Finished size: Depth 8", repeat interval 1 ¾".

Yarn: DMC Cebelia 30 (100% cotton; 515m/50g): white.

Needles: Size 1 (2.4 mm).

Notions: Size 22 tapestry needle.

Repeat from Row 1 for length desired.

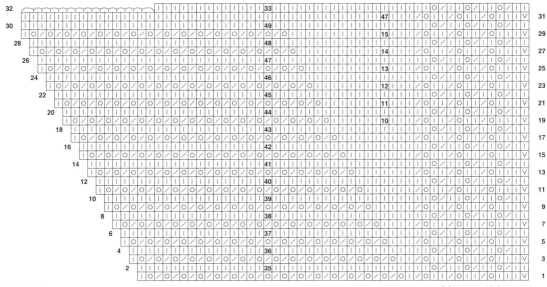

Wide Edging

CO 46 sts. Knit 1 row.

CO 46 sts. Knit 1 row.

Row 1: Sl 1, k3, (yo, k2tog, k2) 2 times, yo, k2tog, k1, (yo, k2tog) 15 times, yo, k1—47 sts.

Row 2: K35, (yo, k2tog, k2) 3 times.

Row 3: Sl 1, k3, (yo, k2tog, k2) 3 times, (yo, k2tog) 15 times, yo, k1—48 sts.

Row 4: K36, (yo, k2tog, k2) 3 times.

Row 5: Sl 1, k3, (yo, k2tog, k2) 3 times, k1, (yo, k2tog) 15 times, yo, k1—49 sts.

Row 6: K37, (yo, k2tog, k2) 3 times.

Row 7: Sl 1, k3, (yo, k2tog, k2) 3 times, k2, (yo, k2tog) 15 times, yo, k1—50 sts.

Row 8: K38, (yo, k2tog, k2) 3 times.

Row 9: Sl 1, k3, (yo, k2tog, k2) 3 times, k3, (yo, k2tog) 15 times, yo, k1—51 sts.

Row 10: K39, (yo, k2tog, k2) 3 times.

Row 11: Sl 1, k3, (yo, k2tog, k2) 3 times, k4, (yo, k2tog) 15 times, yo, k1—52 sts.

Row 12: K40, (yo, k2tog, k2) 3 times.

Row 13: Sl 1, k3, (yo, k2tog, k2) 3 times, k5, (yo, k2tog) 15 times, yo, k1—53 sts.

Row 14: K41, (yo, k2tog, k2) 3 times.

Row 15: Sl 1, k3, (yo, k2tog, k2) 3 times, k6, (yo, k2tog) 15 times, yo, k1—54 sts.

Row 16: K42, (yo, k2tog, k2) 3 times.

Row 17: Sl 1, k3, (yo, k2tog, k2) 3 times, k7, (yo, k2tog) 15 times, yo, k1—55 sts.

Row 18: K43, (yo, k2tog, k2) 3 times.

Row 19: Sl 1, k3, (yo, k2tog, k2) 3 times, k8, (yo, k2tog) 15 times, yo, k1—56 sts.

Row 20: K44, (yo, k2tog, k2) 3 times.

Row 21: Sl 1, k3, (yo, k2tog, k2) 3 times, k9, (yo, k2tog) 15 times, yo, k1—57 sts.

Row 22: K45, (yo, k2tog, k2) 3 times.

Row 23: Sl 1, k3, (yo, k2tog, k2) 3 times, k10, (yo, k2tog) 15 times, yo, k1—58 sts.

Row 24: K46, (yo, k2tog, k2) 3 times.

Row 25: Sl 1, k3, (yo, k2tog, k2) 3 times, k11, (yo, k2tog) 15 times, yo, k1—59 sts.

Row 26: K47, (yo, k2tog, k2) 3 times.

Row 27: Sl 1, k3, (yo, k2tog, k2) 3 times, k12, (yo, k2tog) 15 times, yo, k1—60 sts.

Row 28: K48, (yo, k2tog, k2) 3 times.

Row 29: Sl 1, k3, (yo, k2tog, k2) 3 times, k13, (yo, k2tog) 15 times, yo, k1—61 sts.

Row 30: K49, (yo, k2tog, k2) 3 times.

Row 31: Sl 1, k3, (yo, k2tog, k2) 2 times, yo, k2tog, k47—61 sts.

Row 32: BO 15, k33, (yo, k2tog, k2) 3 times—46 sts.

Repeat Rows 1–32 for 23 repeats total.

Finishing: Graft beginning and ending edges together.

— · — · — · — · — · — · — · — · —

Christening Dress—Narrow Insertion

Narrow Insertion is used down the center of the front yoke.

Finished size: Depth 3 ½", repeat interval 1 ¼".

Yarn: DMC Cebelia 30 (100% cotton; 515m/50g): white.

Needles: Size 1 (2.4 mm).

CO 33 sts. Knit 1 row.

Set-up Row A: Sl 1, (k2, yo, k2tog) 2 times, k1, (yo, k2tog) 5 times, k6, yo, k2tog, k2, yo, k2tog, k1.

Set-up Row B: Sl 1, (k2, yo, k2tog) 2 times, k17, yo, k2tog, k2, yo, k2tog, k1.

Row 1: Sl 1, (k2, yo, k2tog) 2 times, k2, (yo, k2tog) 5 times, k5, yo, k2tog, k2, yo, k2tog, k1.

Row 2 and all even rows: Sl 1, (k2,

Repeat from Row 1 for length desired.

```
| / O | | / O | | | | | | / O / O / O / O / O | / O | | / O | | V   15
| / O | | / O | | | | | / O / O / O / O / O | | / O | | / O | | V    13
| / O | | / O | | | | / O / O / O / O / O | | | / O | | / O | | V    11
| / O | | / O | | | / O / O / O / O / O | | | | / O | | / O | | V    9
| / O | | / O | | / O / O / O / O / O | | | | | / O | | / O | | V    7
| / O | | / O | | | / O / O / O / O / O | | | | / O | | / O | | V    5
| / O | | / O | | | | / O / O / O / O / O | | | / O | | / O | | V    3
| / O | | / O | | | | | | | | | | | | | | | | | / O | | / O | | V    1

B  V | | O / | | O / | | | | | | | | | | | | | | | | | | | O / | | O / |      Set-up rows
   | / O | | / O | | | | | / O / O / O / O / O | | / O | | / O | | V   A
```

Narrow Insertion   CO 33 sts. Knit 1 row.

Even rows: S1 1, (k2, yo, k2tog) 2 times, k17, yo, k2tog, k2, yo k2tog, k1.

yo, k2tog) 2 times, k17, yo, k2tog, k2, yo, k2tog, k1.

Row 3: Sl 1, (k2, yo, k2tog) 2 times, k3, (yo, k2tog) 5 times, k4, yo, k2tog, k2, yo, k2tog, k1.

Row 5: Sl 1, (k2, yo, k2tog) 2 times, k4, (yo, k2tog) 5 times, k3, yo, k2tog, k2, yo, k2tog, k1.

Row 7: Sl 1, (k2, yo, k2tog) 2 times, k5, (yo, k2tog) 5 times, k2, yo, k2tog, k2, yo, k2tog, k1.

Row 9: Sl 1, (k2, yo, k2tog) 2 times, k4, (yo, k2tog) 5 times, k3, yo, k2tog, k2, yo, k2tog, k1.

Row 11: Sl 1, (k2, yo, k2tog) 2 times, k3, (yo, k2tog) 5 times, k4, yo, k2tog, k2, yo, k2tog, k1.

Row 13: Sl 1, (k2, yo, k2tog) 2 times, k2, (yo, k2tog) 5 times, k5, yo, k2tog, k2, yo, k2tog, k1.

Row 15: Sl 1, (k2, yo, k2tog) 2 times, k1, (yo, k2tog) 5 times, k6, yo, k2tog, k2, yo, k2tog, k1.

Row 16: Sl 1, (k2, yo, k2tog) 2 times, k17, yo, k2tog, k2, yo, k2tog, k1.

Repeat Rows 1–16 for 4 repeats total.

---·---·---·---·---·---·---

Christening Dress— Wide Insertion

Wide Insertion is used between tucks on the skirt. It goes around the skirt.

Finished size: Depth 4 ½", repeat interval 1 ¾".

Yarn: DMC Cebelia 30 (100% cotton; 515m/50g): white.

Needles: Size 1 (2.4mm).

Notions: Size 22 tapestry needle.

CO 39 sts. Knit 1 row.

Set-up Row A: Sl 1, (k2, yo, k2tog) 2 times, k1, (yo, k2tog) 7 times, k8, yo, k2tog, k2, yo, k2tog, k1.

Set-up Row B: Sl 1, (k2, yo, k2tog) 2 times, k23, yo, k2tog, k2, yo, k2tog, k1.

Row 1: Sl 1, (k2, yo, k2tog) 2 times, k2, (yo, k2tog) 7 times, k7, yo, k2tog, k2, yo, k2tog, k1.

Row 2 and all even rows: Sl 1, (k2, yo, k2tog) 2 times, k23, yo, k2tog, k2, yo, k2tog, k1.

Row 3: Sl 1, (k2, yo, k2tog) 2 times, k3, (yo, k2tog) 7 times, k6, yo, k2tog, k2, yo, k2tog, k1.

Row 5: Sl 1, (k2, yo, k2tog) 2 times, k4, (yo, k2tog) 7 times, k5, yo, k2tog, k2, yo, k2tog, k1.

Row 7: Sl 1, (k2, yo, k2tog) 2 times, k5, (yo, k2tog) 7 times, k4, yo, k2tog, k2, yo, k2tog, k1.

Row 9: Sl 1, (k2, yo, k2tog) 2 times, k6, (yo, k2tog) 7 times, k3, yo, k2tog, k2, yo, k2tog, k1.

Row 11: Sl 1, (k2, yo, k2tog) 2 times, k7, (yo, k2tog) 7 times, k2, yo, k2tog, k2, yo, k2tog, k1.

Row 13: Sl 1, (k2, yo, k2tog) 2 times, k6, (yo, k2tog) 7 times, k3, yo, k2tog, k2, yo, k2tog, k1.

Row 15: Sl 1, (k2, yo, k2tog) 2 times, k5, (yo, k2tog) 7 times, k4, yo, k2tog, k2, yo, k2tog, k1.

Row 17: Sl 1, (k2, yo, k2tog) 2 times, k4, (yo, k2tog) 7 times, k5, yo, k2tog, k2, yo, k2tog, k1.

Row 19: Sl 1, (k2, yo, k2tog) 2 times, k3, (yo, k2tog) 7 times, k6, yo, k2tog, k2, yo, k2tog, k1.

Row 21: Sl 1, (k2, yo, k2tog) 2 times, k2, (yo, k2tog) 7 times, k7, yo, k2tog, k2, yo, k2tog, k1.

Row 23: Sl 1, (k2, yo, k2tog) 2 times, k1, (yo, k2tog) 7 times, k8, yo, k2tog, k2, yo, k2tog, k1.

Row 24: Sl 1, (k2, yo, k2tog) 2 times, k23, yo, k2tog, k2, yo, k2tog, k1.

Repeat Rows 1–24 for 28 repeats total.

Finishing: Graft beginning and ending edges together.

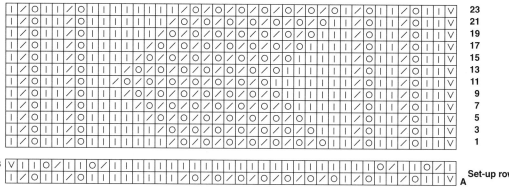

Wide Insertion

CO 39 sts. Knit 1 row.

Even rows: Sl 1, (k2, yo, k2tog) 2 times, k23, yo, k2tog, k2, yo, k2tog, k1.

Very Narrow Lace

I don't suppose this lace is unique. I sat down at a conference and simply knit it, without any directions.

Very Narrow Lace is used to edge the slip for the christening gown. It would be equally pretty on a handkerchief or lingerie.

Finished size: Depth ¾", repeat interval ½".

Yarn: DMC Cordonnet 30 (100% cotton; 197m/20g): white.

Needles: Size 1 (2.4 mm).

CO 6 sts. Knit 1 row.

Row 1: Sl 1, k1, yo, k2tog, yo twice, k2—8 sts.

Row 2: K3, p1, k4.

Row 3: Sl 1, k1, yo, k2tog, k4.

Row 4: Knit.

Row 5: Sl 1, k1, yo, (k2tog, yo twice) 2 times, k2—11 sts.

Row 6: K3, p1, k2, p1, k4.

Row 7: Sl 1, k1, yo, k2tog, k7.

Row 8: BO 5, k5—6 sts.

Repeat Rows 1–8 for desired length.

Repeat from Row 1 for length desired.

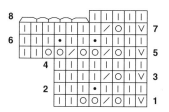

CO 6 sts. Knit 1 row.

BERNADIN'S SAMPLER

These knitting patterns were mastered by Bernadin Loeffler, age ten, who made the sampler in 1870. It is composed of ten different knitted grounds. The sampler is owned by the Laura Ingalls Wilder Museum, Mansfield, Missouri.

Wreaths Ground—Bernadin's Sampler #5

Bernadin's Sampler was published in Woman's Day *magazine in October 1961. You sent in fifty cents for the written patterns. I named this one "Wreaths". The sample shows two edge stitches on each side.*

Finished size: Depth 1 ½", repeat interval 2".
Yarn: DMC Cebelia 10 (100% cotton; 260m/50g): ecru.
Needles: Size 2 (2.8 mm).

CO multiple of 9 sts.
Set-up Row A: *Yo, ssk, k5, k2tog, repeat from *, end last repeat yo.
Set-up Row B: Purl.
Row 1: *K1, yo, ssk, k3, k2tog, yo, repeat from *, end last repeat k1.
Row 2 and all even rows: Purl.
Row 3: *K2, yo, ssk, k1, k2tog, yo, k1, repeat from *, end last repeat k2.

Row 5: K2tog, yo, k5, yo, *sl 2 tog, k1, p2sso, yo, k5, yo; repeat from *, end last repeat yo, ssk.

Row 7: *K4, yo, ssk, k2, repeat from *, end last repeat k3.

Row 9: *K2, k2tog, yo, k1, yo, ssk, k1, repeat from *, end last repeat k2.

Row 11: *K1, k2tog, yo, k3, yo, ssk, repeat from *, end last repeat k1.

Row 13: *K3, yo, sl 2tog k-wise, k1, p2sso, yo, k2, repeat from *, end last repeat k3.

Row 15: *Yo, ssk, k6, repeat from *, end last repeat yo, ssk, k5, k2tog, yo.

Row 16: Purl.

Finishing: Repeat Rows 1–16 for length desired.

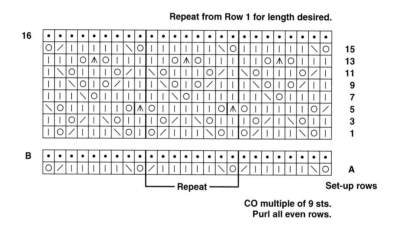

Repeat from Row 1 for length desired.

CO multiple of 9 sts.
Purl all even rows.

Perky Leaves Ground—Bernadin's Sampler #11

I named this pattern from Bernadin's Sampler "Perky Leaves". The sample shows two edge stitches on each side.

Finished size: Depth 1 ¼", repeat interval 1 ¾".

Yarn: DMC Cebelia 10 (100% cotton; 260 m/50 g): ecru.

Needles: Size 2 (2.8 mm).

CO multiple of 10 + 1 sts.

Row 1: *K1, yo, ssk, k5, k2tog, yo, repeat from *, end last repeat k1.

Row 2 and all even rows: Purl.

Row 3: *K1, yo, k1, ssk, k3, k2tog, k1, yo, repeat from *, end last repeat k1.

Row 5: *K1, yo, k2, ssk, k1, k2tog, k2, yo, repeat from *, end last repeat k1.

Row 7: *K1, yo, k3, sl 2tog k-wise, k1, p2sso, k3, yo, repeat from *, end last repeat k1.

Row 9: *K3, k2tog, yo, k1, yo, ssk, k2, repeat from *, end last repeat k3.

Row 11: *K2, k2tog, (k1, yo) 2 times, k1, ssk, k1, repeat from *, end last repeat k2.

Row 13: *K1, k2tog, k2, yo, k1, yo, k2, ssk, repeat from *, end last repeat k1.

Row 15: K2tog, k3, yo, k1, yo, k3, * sl 2tog k-wise, k1, p2sso, k3, yo, k1, yo, k3, repeat from *, end last repeat ssk.

Row 16. Purl.

Finishing: Repeat Rows 1–16 for length desired.

Repeat from Row 1 for length desired.

— Repeat —

CO multiple of 10 + 1 sts.
Purl all even rows.

Frank Notes on the Knitting in the Stamford Historical Society

October 27, 1960. These are notes I made on knitted pieces in the Stamford Historical Society, Stamford, Connecticut. Rose Wilder Lane arranged for me to write out the patterns in connection with her *Woman's Day* article on knitted lace.

As knitted lace goes, this is new rather than of high value. Bar the cuff, the stocking, and the Double Diamond pattern, which are fairly staple material, the rest have a family likeness, which makes me think they are by the same knitter, and the result of her own adaptations. The other pieces may or may not be knitted by the same woman, but they are knitted by patterns already familiar to me.

The family likeness includes a predication [sic] for (a) the buttonhole effect, (b) herringbone fagoting in doubles and triples, (c) loop edges, and (d) a general rococo effect.

She knitted in fine and medium weights of cotton, and with few errors—I have had occasion to examine her pieces rather closely! But her chief virtue is her willingness to experiment. None of these items is run-of-the-mill. I am glad to add each of them to my collection. She knows not only each of the stitches (like knowing one's letters) but the usual units of design, which are like words. And then she makes them into an entirely new sentence. But in an effort to be poetic, she uses too many adjectives. In knitting terms, she uses lace stitches a very large proportion of the time, and the effect is too fussy. Therefore none of these patterns is a candidate for my list of patterns which I knit over and over again.

Double Diamond Edging
(Shown on page 34.)

The best of the lot, it is easy, though the directions don't look it. It is also easy to remember, as things follow logically.

Finished size: Depth 4", repeat interval 1 ½"
Yarn: DMC Cordonnet 30 (100% cotton; 197m/20g): white.
Needles: Size 1 (2.4 mm).

CO 29 sts. Knit 1 row.
Row 1: Sl 1, k2, yo, k2tog, k5, k2tog, yo, (k1, yo, ssk) 2 times, k3, (k2tog, yo, k1) 2 times, yo, k2—30 sts.
Row 2 and all even-numbered rows: Knit.
Row 3: Sl 1, k2, yo, k2tog, k4, k2tog, yo, k3, (yo, ssk, k1) 2 times, k2tog, yo, k1, k2tog, yo, k3, yo, k2—31 sts.
Row 5: Sl 1, k2, yo, k2tog, k3, k2tog, yo, k5, yo, ssk, k1, yo, sl 2tog k-wise, k1, p2sso, yo, k1, k2tog, yo, k5, yo, k2—32 sts.
Row 7: Sl 1, k2, yo, k2tog, k2, (k2tog, yo, k1) 2 times, (yo, ssk, k1) 2 times, k2, (k2tog, yo, k1) 2 times, yo, ssk, k1, yo, k2—33 sts.

Row 9: Sl 1, k2, yo, k2tog, k1, (k2tog, yo, k1) 2 times, k2, (yo, ssk, k1) 2 times, (k2tog, yo, k1) 2 times, k2, yo, ssk, k1, yo, k2—34 sts.

Row 11: Sl 1, k2, yo, (k2tog) 2 times, yo, k1, k2tog, yo, k5, yo, ssk, k1, yo, sl 2tog k-wise, k1, p2sso, yo, k1, k2tog, yo k5, yo, ssk, k1, yo, k2—35 sts.

Row 13: Sl 1, k2, yo, k2tog, (k1, yo, ssk) 2 times, k3, k2tog, yo, k1, k2tog, yo, (k1, yo, ssk) 2 times, k3, (k2tog, yo, k1) 2 times, k1.

Row 15: Sl 1, k2, yo, k2tog, k2, (yo, ssk, k1) 2 times, (k2tog, yo, k1) 2 times, k2, (yo, ssk, k1) 2 times, (k2tog, yo, k1) 2 times, k2.

Row 17: Sl 1, k2, yo, k2tog, k3, yo, ssk, k1, yo, sl 2tog k-wise, k1, p2sso, yo, k1, k2tog, yo, k5, yo, ssk, k1, yo, sl 2tog k-wise, k1, p2sso, yo, k1, k2tog, yo, k4.

Row 19: Sl 1, k2, yo, k2tog, k4, yo, ssk, k3, (k2tog, yo, k1) 2 times, (yo, ssk, k1) 2 times, k2, k2tog, yo, k5.

Row 21: Sl 1, k2, yo, k2tog, k5, yo, ssk, k1, (k2tog, yo, k1) 2 times, k2, (yo, ssk, k1) 2 times, k2tog, yo, k6.

Row 23: Sl 1, k2, yo, k2tog, k6, yo, sl 2tog k-wise, k1, p2sso, yo, k1, k2tog, yo, k5, yo, ssk, k1, yo, sl 2tog k-wise, k1, p2sso, yo, k7.

Row 24: BO 6 sts, knit across—29 sts.

Finishing: Repeat Rows 1–24 for length desired.

Repeat from Row 1 for length desired.

CO 29 sts. Knit 1 row.
Knit all even rows.

MY FAVORITE PATTERN

Apassionate collector hunts in many places. I hunted through many crochet direction books which occasionally contained a knitted lace pattern or two. I think the store where I searched hated the sight of me!

Since then I have kept my eyes open for patterns anywhere. I have adapted crocheted and bobbin lace patterns, as well as commercially made lace. I even wrote out the directions from a plastic doily!

Heirloom Apron Lace is my favorite lace; I knit it over and over. The basic idea combines the torchon and blank diamond patterns and was adapted from a crocheted original.

Heirloom Apron Lace

Finished size: Depth 4", repeat interval 1 ¼".
Yarn: DMC Cebelia 10 (100% cotton; 260m/50g): ecru.
Needles: Size 2 (2.8 mm).
Gauge: 9 repeats = 12".

CO 30 sts. Knit 1 row.
Row 1: Sl 1, k3, yo, (ssk, k5, k2tog, yo, k3, yo) 2 times, k2—31 sts.
Row 2 and all even rows: Purl, except p1, k1, p1 in "yo 3 times", knit last 2 sts.

Row 3: Sl 1, k4, yo, (ssk, k3, k2tog, yo, k5, yo) 2 times, k2—32 sts.
Row 5: Sl 1, k5, yo, (ssk, k1, k2tog, yo, k7, yo) 2 times, k2—33 sts.
Row 7: Sl 1, k6, yo, sl 2tog k-wise, k1, p2sso, yo, k9, yo, sl 2tog k-

---

Mary's Teaching Notes
Double Decreases

There are three different double decreases that can be used in a pattern. K3tog gives a double decrease with a right slant; sl 2tog k-wise, k1, p2sso gives a centered double decrease; and k3tog tbl gives a double decrease with a left slant. Older patterns do not differentiate between these different methods. The decision as to which to use was, and usually still is, left up to the knitter. There are two different double decreases used in this pattern. The centered double decrease is used at the point of the diamond. It gives a sharp look to the point. The other results in a right slant.

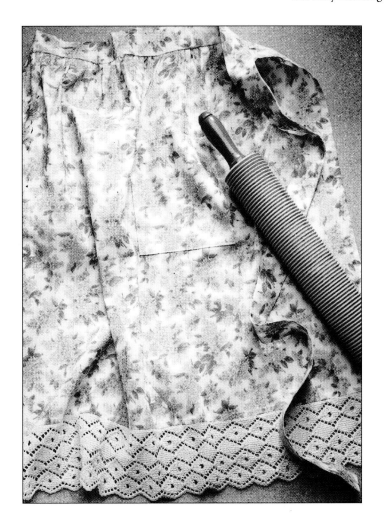

Repeat from Row 1 for length desired. End with Row 6.

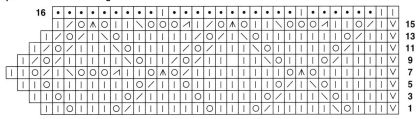

CO 30 sts. Knit 1 row.

Even rows: Purl except p1, k1, p1 in "yo 3 times" and knit last 2 sts.

wise, k1, p2sso, yo, k2, k3tog, yo 3 times, ssk, k2, yo, k2—34 sts.

Row 9: Sl 1, k4, k2tog, yo, (k3, yo, ssk, k5, k2tog, yo) 2 times, k2tog, k1—33 sts.

Row 11: Sl 1, k3, k2tog, yo, (k5, yo, ssk, k3, k2tog, yo) 2 times, k2tog, k1—32 sts.

Row 13: Sl 1, k2, k2tog, yo, (k7, yo, ssk, k1, k2tog, yo) 2 times, k2tog, k1—31 sts.

Row 15: Sl 1, k1, k2tog, yo, (k2, k3tog, yo 3 times, ssk, k2, yo, sl 2tog k-wise, k1, p2sso, yo) 2 times, k2tog, k1—30 sts.

Row 16: Purl across to within 2 sts of end, k2.

Finishing: Repeat Rows 1–16 for length desired. End with Row 6.

Heirloom Apron Insertion

Finished size: Depth 4", repeat interval 1 ¾".

Yarn: DMC Cebelia 10 (100% cotton; 260m/50g): ecru.

Needles: Size 2 (2.8 mm).

CO 27 sts. Knit 1 row.

Row 1: Sl 1, k2tog, yo, k2, k2tog, yo 3 times, k3tog tbl, k2, yo, sl 2tog k-wise, k1, p2sso, yo, k2, k2tog, yo 3 times, k3tog tbl, k2, yo, ssk, k1.

Row 2 and all even rows: Sl 1, purl to last st, k1, except p1, k1, p1 in "yo 3 times".

Row 3: Sl 1, k2, (yo, ssk, k5, k2tog, yo, k3) 2 times.

Row 5: Sl 1, k3, yo, ssk, k3, k2tog, yo, k5, yo, ssk, k3, k2tog, yo, k4.

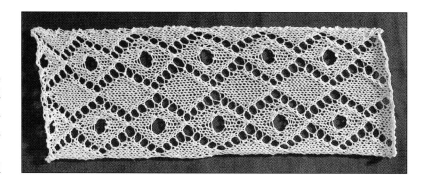

Repeat from Row 1 for length desired.

CO 27 sts. Knit 1 row.
Even rows: Sl 1, purl to last st, k1.
P1, k1, p1 in "yo 3 times".

Row 7: Sl 1, k4, yo, ssk, k1, k2tog, yo, k7, yo, ssk, k1, k2tog, yo, k5.

Row 9: Sl 1, k5, yo, sl 2tog k-wise, k1, p2sso, yo, k9, yo, sl 2tog k-wise, k1, p2sso, yo, k6.

Row 11: Sl 1, k3, k2tog, yo, k3, yo, ssk, k5, k2tog, yo, k3, yo, ssk, k4.

Row 13: Sl 1, k2, k2tog, yo, k5, yo, ssk, k3, k2tog, yo, k5, yo, ssk, k3.

Row 15: Sl 1, k1, k2tog, yo, k7, yo, ssk, k1, k2tog, yo, k7, yo, ssk, k2.

Row 16: Sl 1, purl to last st, k1.

Finishing: Repeat Rows 1–16 for length desired.

AMATEUR ASTRONOMERS ASSOCIATION

My other hobby that I am passionate about is astronomy. My happiest childhood memories are of summer evenings when my mother would let me stay up late and show me the stars.

Starting in 1952, I arranged for ten lecturers a year for over twenty-five years for the Recent Advances in Astronomy series taught by the Amateur Astronomers Association. I got to know many famous people, among them Harold Urey, Nobel Prize winner for his work in physics in 1933.

I dreamed up a five-pointed star to send as a thank-you to the lecturers at Christmas time. Some of the lecturers were Jewish, so I also invented a six-pointed star.

Christmas Star

The star center is started like a doily. I wired the points to keep the star's shape. You could mount it in a ring instead.

Finished size: 6 ½" point to point.

Yarn: J & P Coats, Knit-Cro-Sheen (85% cotton, 15% metallic; 100 yds): various colors, ⅓ ball. YLI, Candlelight (65% rayon, 35% polyester; 75 yds): color to match metallic thread in Knit-Cro-Sheen.

Needles: Size 1 (2.4 mm): set of 4 dpn.

Notions: Size 10 crochet hook, size 22 tapestry needle, 22 gauge brass wire, needle-nose pliers.

• **Center:** CO 5 sts on 3 needles, 2 on needle 1, 2 on needle 2, and 1 on needle 3. Knit 1 rnd.

Rnd 1: Knit in front and back of each st—10 sts.

Rnd 2: Knit.

Rnd 3: *K1, yo, k1, repeat from *—15 sts.

Rnd 4: Knit.

Rnd 5: Knit.

Rnd 6: *K1, (yo, k1) 2 times, repeat from *—25 sts.

Rnd 7: Knit.

Rnd 8: Knit.

Rnd 9: *K1, yo, k3, yo, k1, repeat from *—35 sts.

Rnd 10: Knit.

Rnd 11: Knit.

Rnd 12: *K1, yo, k5, yo, k1, repeat from *—45 sts.

Rnd 13: Knit.

Rnd 14: Knit.

Rnd 15: *K1, yo, k1, (yo, k2tog) 3 times, yo, k1, repeat from *—55 sts.

Rnd 16: Knit, ending row with knit

in front and back of st.

•**Point:** Instructions are for one point. Repeat for other four points, working each point separately.

Row 1: K2, p1, turn for first point only. K1, p1, turn for other 4 points.

Row 2: Sl 1, yo, k2, turn.

Row 3: K2, p3, turn.

Row 4: Sl 1, k4, turn.

Row 5: K2, p4, turn.

Row 6: Sl 1, k3, yo, k2, turn.

Row 7: K2, p6, turn.

Row 8: Sl 1, k7, turn.

Row 9: K2, p7, turn.

Row 10: Sl 1, k6, yo, k2, turn.

Row 11: K2, p9, turn.

Row 12: Sl 1, k10, turn.

Row 13: K2, p10, turn.

Row 14: Sl 1, k9, yo, k2, turn.

Row 15: K2, p12, turn.

Row 16: Sl 1, k13, turn.

Row 17: K2, p13, turn.

Row 18: Sl 1, (yo, k2tog, k1) 4 times, yo, k2.

Star of David and Christmas star.

Row 19: K17, turn.
Row 20: Sl 1, k16.
Row 21: BO 16 sts loosely.

Finishing: Bend wire into a star shape with each side 2 ½" long. Twist ends together. Hold point of star inside wire and work two crochet sts in each knit st and over wire all around edge of star. One side of point will have 18 sts and the other side 24 sts. Block. Apply spray starch and press with iron.

Star of David

I created this in 1969. Wire the points or mount in a ring.

Finished size: 7" point to point.

Yarn: J & P Coats, Knit-Cro-Sheen (85% cotton, 15% metallic; 100yds): white with silver, color 108 blue OR DMC Cebelia 10 (100% cotton; 260m/50g): white, color 799 blue.

Needles: Size 2 (2.8 mm) set of 4 dpn.

Notions: Size 10 crochet hook, size 22 tapestry needle, 22 gauge brass wire, needle-nose pliers.

CO 6 sts, 2 sts each on 3 needles. Knit 1 rnd.
Rnd 1: *Knit in front and back of each st—12 sts.
Rnd 2: Knit.
Rnd 3: *K1, yo, k1, repeat from *—18 sts.
Rnd 4: Knit.
Rnd 5: Knit.
Rnd 6: *K1, (yo, k1) 2 times, repeat from *—30 sts.
Rnd 7: Knit.
Rnd 8: Knit.
Rnd 9: *K1, yo, k3, yo, k1, repeat from *—42 sts.
Rnd 10: Knit.
Rnd 11: Knit.
Rnd 12: *K1, yo, ssk, k1, k2tog, yo, k1, repeat from *.
Rnd 13: Knit.
Rnd 14: Knit.
Rnd 15: *K1, yo, k5, yo, k1, repeat from *—54 sts.
Rnd 16: Knit.
Rnd 17: Knit.
Rnd 18: *(K1, yo) 2 times, (k2tog, yo) 3 times, k1, rep from *—66 sts.
Do not cut white. With blue:
Rnd 19: Knit.
Rnd 20: Knit.
Rnd 21: Knit.

Rnd 22: Knit.
Cut blue thread, tie ends into a granny knot.

•Point: Pick up white thread.
knit 2, p1, turn. (First point only.)
Row 2: Sl 1, k2, turn.
Row 3: K2, p2, turn.
Row 4: Sl 1, k3, turn.
Row 5: K2, p3, turn.
Row 6: Sl 1, k4, turn.
Row 7: K2, p4, turn.
Row 8: Sl 1, k1, k2tog, yo, k2, turn.
Row 9: K2, p5, turn.
Row 10: Sl 1, k6, turn.
Row 11: K2, p6, turn.
Row 12: Sl 1, k3, k2tog, yo, k2, turn.
Row 13: K2, p7, turn.
Row 14: Sl 1, k8, turn.
Row 15: K2, p8, turn.
Row 16: Sl 1, k2, yo, k2tog, k1, (yo, k2) 2 times, turn.
Row 17: K13, turn.
Row 18: Sl 1, k12, turn.

Row 19: Loosely BO 13 sts, k1, p1. Repeat rows 2–19 for other 5 points. Last point join with first point.

Finishing: Untie granny knot.

Weave in all 4 ends. Bend wire into a star shape with side of each arm 2 ¼" long. Twist ends together. Hold point of star inside wire and work two crochet sts in each knit st and over

wire all around edge of point. One side of point will require more sts than the other. Block so that the blue sts form lines. Apply spray starch and press with iron.

STARS IN MY HEART

The U.S. space program was in the headlines constantly in the early 1960s. Sheppard and Grissom both made suborbital flights in 1961 and President John F. Kennedy announced plans to land a man on the moon. Interest in astronomy grew as a result. In February 1962, *The Ladies Home Journal* ran an article about me and my love of astronomy called "Stars in My Heart".

"Astronomy has taught me more than I can ever put into words. I have known wonder and delight, standing in happy humility before the magnitude of the things God has made. I have learned to feel in every nerve and bone that the turning Earth—and I on this Earth—is part of the hosts of heaven, of the billions of stars inhabiting billions of galaxies for billions of years. I have learned to accept the evidence that planets, sunsets, atmosphere, chickweed, and human beings are, in some curious way, byproducts of a more intricate and magnificent drama—the history of stars!"

Veil Nebula Edging

I invented this edging on March 31, 1955. I had just read Hoyle's new book Frontiers in Astronomy. *I had also read his recent papers theorizing on the formation of giant stars.*

A nebula is a cloud of glowing gas and dust in the heavens. The Veil Nebula is the result of a supernova in the Cygnus constellation.

Finished size: Depth 2", repeat interval 1".
Yarn: DMC Cebelia 30 (100% cotton; 515m/50g): white.
Needles: Size 1 (2.4 mm).

Note: Keep the "yo" at the beginning of the even rows fairly loose.

CO 19 sts. Knit 1 row.

Row 1: Sl 1, k1, (yo, k2tog) 2 times, yo, k3, (yo, k2tog) 2 times, (yo, sl 2tog k-wise, k1, p2sso) 2 times—18 sts.
Row 2: Yo, k16, yo, k2tog—19 sts.
Row 3: Sl 1, k1, (yo, k2tog) 2 times, yo, ssk, k1, k2tog, (yo, k2tog) 2 times, yo, sl 2 tog k-wise, k2tog, p2sso—16 sts.
Row 4: Yo, k14, yo, k2tog—17 sts.
Row 5: Sl 1, k1, (yo, k2tog)

2 times, k1, yo, sl 2tog k-wise, k1, p2sso, yo, k3, (yo, k2tog) 2 times.

Row 6: Yo, k15, yo, k2tog—18 sts.

Row 7: Sl 1, k1, (yo, k2tog) 2 times, k1, yo, k2tog, yo, ssk, k1, k2tog, (yo, k2tog) 2 times—17 sts.

Row 8: Yo, k15, yo, k2tog.

Row 9: Sl 1, k1, (yo, k2tog) 4 times, yo, sl 2tog k-wise, k1, p2sso, yo, k3, yo, k2tog.

Row 10: Yo, k16, yo, k2tog—19 sts.

Row 11: Sl 1, k1, yo, k2tog, yo, k3tog, (yo, k2tog) 2 times, yo,

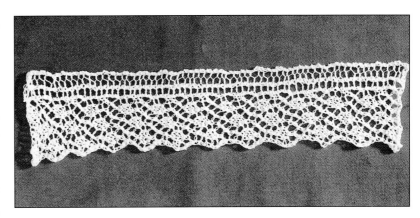

k1, yo, ssk, k1, k2tog, yo, k2tog—18 sts.

Row 12: Yo, k16, yo, k2tog—19 sts.

Finishing: Repeat Rows 1–12 for length desired.

Repeat from Row 1 for length desired.

▣ S1 2tog k-wise, k2tog, p2sso

CO 19 sts. Knit 1 row.

Keep the "yo" at beginning of even rows fairly loose.

Loop Nebula Doily

Finished size: 11" diameter.

Yarn: DMC Cebelia 10 (100% cotton; 260m/50g): white.

Needles: Size 2 (2.8 mm): set of 4 4 dpn, circular.

Notions: Size 5 crochet hook.

Notes: All directions are to be repeated six times. All odd rows except 3, 7, and 35: knit, but k1,

Loop Nebula Doily.

p1 in "yo twice". See instructions for Rows 3, 7 and 35.

CO 6 sts on 3 needles.
Rnd 1: Knit—6 sts.
Rnd 2: Knit.
Rnd 3: Yo, k1—18 sts.
Rnd 4: Knit.
Rnd 6: Knit.
Rnd 7: (Yo, k1) 2 times—24 sts.
Rnd 8: Knit.
Rnd 10: Knit.
Rnd 12: K2tog, yo twice, ssk.
Rnd 14: K2, yo twice, k2—36 sts.
Rnd 16: K3, yo twice, k3—48 sts.

Rnd 18: Yo, k2, k2tog, yo twice, ssk, k2—54 sts.
Rnd 20: Yo, k1, yo, k2, k2tog, yo twice, ssk, k2—66 sts.
Rnd 22: Yo, k2tog, yo, k1, yo, k2, k2tog, yo twice, ssk, k2—78 sts.
Rnd 24: (Yo, k2tog) 2 times, yo, k1, yo, k2, k2tog, yo twice, ssk, k2—90 sts.
Rnd 26: Yo, k1, (yo, k2tog) 3 times yo, k2, k2tog, yo twice, ssk, k2—102 sts.
Rnd 28: Yo, k1, (yo, k2tog) 4 times, yo, k2, k2tog, yo twice, ssk, k2—114 sts.

Rnd 30: Yo, k1, (yo, k2tog) 5 times, yo, k2, k2tog, yo twice, ssk, k2—126 sts.
Rnd 32: K15, k2tog, yo twice, ssk, k2.
Rnd 34: K16, yo, k2tog, yo, k3—132 sts.
Rnd 35: Sl 3 sts of each needle onto right-hand needle. Knit.
Rnd 36: (Yo, k1, yo, k2tog) 6 times, (yo, k1) 2 times, yo, k2tog—30 sts.
Rnd 38: (K3, yo, sl 2tog k-wise, k1, p2sso, yo) 5 times.
Rnd 40: (Yo, sl 2tog k-wise, k1,

p2sso, yo, k3) 5 times.

Rnd 42: (K3, yo, sl 2tog k-wise, k1, p2sso, yo) 5 times.

Rnd 44: (Yo, sl 2tog k-wise, k1, p2sso, yo, k3) 5 times.

Rnd 46: (K3, yo, sl 2tog k-wise, k1, p2sso, yo) 5 times.

Rnd 48: (Yo, sl 2tog k-wise, k1, p2sso, yo, k3) 5 times.

Rnd 49: Knit.

With crochet hook, sc in 3 sts tog, ch 6. Repeat around. Join in first sc. Sl st to center of loop. Ch 6 around. Fasten off.

Finishing: Block to 11" diameter.

See written instruction for crochet finishing.

Chart row numbers (top to bottom): 48, 46, 44, 42, 40, 38, 36, 35, 34, 32, 30, 28, 26, 24, 22, 20, 18, 16, 14, 12, 10, 8, 7, 6, 4, 3, 2, 1

Row 35: Sl 3 sts to the right

CO 6 sts on 3 needles.
Odd rnds: Knit, except k1, p1 in "yo twice".
Follow instruction for Rows 3, 7 and 35.

Repeat 6 times

LACE EVERYWHERE

I see lace everywhere I look. When I lived in Norman, Texas, I went on an arranged bus trip to Southern Methodist University's Meadows Museum to look at art. I can't paint anything, I'm completely unartistic. But when we came to this painting, I hung back from the group to take notes on the petticoat lace. I wrote out the instructions at home later.

The painting is *Girl Removing Her Garter* by Antonio Maria Esquivel, 1842. The petticoat has bobbin lace of which the following is a knitted version.

Esquivel Lace

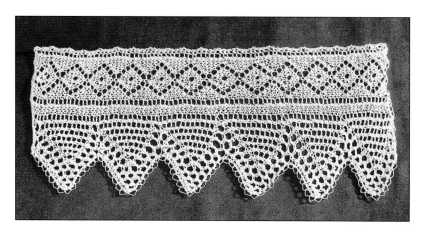

Finished size: Depth 4", repeat interval 1 ¾".

Yarn: DMC Cordonnet 30 (100% cotton; 197m/20g): white.

Needles: Size 0 (2.1 mm).

CO 30 sts. Knit 1 row.

Row 1: Sl 1, k1, yo, k2tog, k3, k2tog, yo, k1, yo, ssk, k3, yo, k2tog, k2, yo, k2tog, k1, k2tog, yo twice, ssk, k2tog, yo twice, k in front and back of st (inc), k1—32 sts.

Row 2: Yo, k2tog, k2, p1, k3, p1, k23.

Row 3: Sl 1, k1, yo, k2tog, k2, k2tog, yo, k3, yo, ssk, k2, yo, k2tog, k2, (yo, k2tog) 2 times, k1, k2tog, yo twice, ssk, k2tog, yo twice, inc, k1—34 sts.

Row 4: Yo, k2tog, k2, p1, k3, p1, k25.

Row 5: Sl 1, k1, yo, k2tog, k1, k2tog, yo, k5, yo, ssk, k1, yo, k2tog, k2, (yo, k2tog) 3 times, k1, k2tog, yo twice, ssk, k2tog, yo twice, inc, k1—36 sts.

Row 6: Yo, k2tog, k2, p1, k3, p1, k27.

Row 7: Sl 1, k1, yo, k2tog twice, yo, k3, yo, ssk, k2, yo, ssk, yo, k2tog, k2, (yo, k2tog) 4 times, k1, k2tog, yo twice, ssk, k2tog, yo twice, inc, k1—38 sts.

Row 8: Yo, k2tog, k2, p1, k3, p1, k29.

Row 9: Sl 1, k1, yo, k2tog, k2, yo, ssk, k3, k2tog, yo, k2, yo, k2tog, k2, (yo, k2tog) 5 times, k1, k2tog, yo twice, ssk, k2tog, yo twice, inc, k1—40 sts.

Row 10: Yo, k2tog, k2, p1, k3, p1, k31.

Row 11: Sl 1, k1, yo, k2tog, k3, yo, ssk, k1, k2tog, yo, k3, yo, k2tog, k2, (yo, k2tog) 6 times, k1, k2tog, yo twice, ssk, k2tog, yo twice, inc, k1—42 sts.

Row 12: Yo, k2tog, k2, p1, k3, p1, k33.

Row 13: Sl 1, k1, yo, k2tog, k4, yo, sl 2tog k-wise, k1, p2sso, yo, k4, yo, k2tog, k2, (yo, k2tog) 7 times, k1, k2tog, yo twice, ssk, k2tog, yo twice, inc, k1—44 sts.

Row 14: Yo, k2tog, k2, p1, k3, p1, k35.

Row 15: Sl 1, k1, yo, k2tog, k3, k2tog, yo, k1, yo, ssk, k3, yo, k2tog, k2, (yo, k2tog) 6 times, k1, (k2tog, yo twice, ssk) 2 times, k2tog, k2—43 sts.

Row 16: Yo, k2tog twice, k1, p1, k3, p1, k33—42 sts.

Row 17: Sl 1, k1, yo, k2tog, k2, k2tog, yo, k3, yo, ssk, k2, yo, k2tog, k2, (yo, k2tog) 5 times, k1, (k2tog, yo twice, ssk) 2 times, k2tog, k2—41 sts.

Row 18: Yo, k2tog twice, k1, p1, k3, p1, k31—40 sts.

Row 19: Sl 1, k1, yo, k2tog, k1, k2tog, yo, k5, yo, ssk, k1, yo, k2tog, k2, (yo, k2tog) 4 times, k1, (k2tog, yo twice, ssk) 2 times, k2tog, k2—39 sts.

Row 20: Yo, k2tog twice, k1, p1, k3, p1, k29—38 sts.

Row 21: Sl 1, k1, yo, k2tog twice, yo, k3, yo, k2tog, k2, yo, ssk, yo, k2tog, k2, (yo, k2tog) 3 times, k1, (k2tog, yo twice, ssk) 2 times, k2tog, k2—37 sts.

Row 22: Yo, k2tog twice, k1, p1, k3, p1, k27—36 sts.

Row 23: Sl 1, k1, yo, k2tog, k2, yo, ssk, k3, k2tog, yo, k2, yo, k2tog, k2, (yo, k2tog) 2 times, k1,

(k2tog, yo twice, ssk) 2 times, k2tog, k2—35 sts.

Row 24: Yo, k2tog twice, k1, p1, k3, p1, k25—34 sts.

Row 25: Sl 1, k1, yo, k2tog, k3, yo, ssk, k1, k2tog, yo, k3, yo, k2tog, k2, yo, k2tog, k1, (k2tog, yo twice, ssk) 2 times, k2tog, k2—33 sts.

Row 26: Yo, k2tog twice, k1, p1,

k3, p1, k23—32 sts.

Row 27: Sl 1, k1, yo, k2tog, k4, yo, sl 2tog k-wise, k1, p2sso, yo, k4, yo, k2tog, k2, (k2tog, yo twice, ssk) 2 times, k2tog, k2—31 sts.

Row 28: Yo, k2tog twice, k1, p1, k3, p1, k21—30 sts.

Finishing: Repeat Rows 1–28 for length desired.

Repeat from Row 1 for length desired.

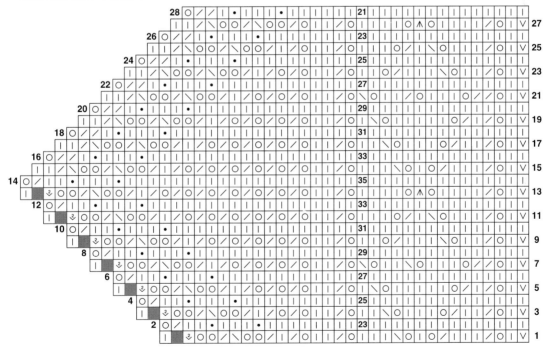

CO 30 sts. Knit 1 row.

OLDE TIME NEEDLEWORK

In 1983, *Olde Time Needlework* published an article about lace knitting and used some of my patterns. I chose ones from my Aunt Jennie's and Aunt Lucy's collections which I had had for over thirty years and which they had probably had for an equally long time.

Laura Brown's Rose-Leaf Lace
(Shown on page 85.)

Finished size: Depth 3 ½", repeat interval ¾".
Yarn: DMC Cebelia 20, (100% cotton; 370m/50g): color 224.
Needles: Size 0 (2.1 mm), size 1 (2.4 mm).

CO 31 sts. Knit 1 row.
Row 1: Sl 1, k3, yo, k2tog, k1, yo, k1, k2tog, p1, ssk, k1, yo, p1, yo, k1, k2tog, p1, ssk, k1, yo, k3, yo, (k2tog, yo twice) 2 times, k2—34 sts.
Row 2: K3, (p1, k2) 2 times, yo, k2tog, p4, k1, (p3, k1) 2 times, p6, yo, k2tog, k2.
Row 3: Sl 1, k3, yo, k2tog, k1, yo, k1, k2tog, p1, ssk, k1, p1, k1, k2tog, p1, ssk, k1, yo, k3, yo, k2tog, k7—32 sts.
Row 4: K9, yo, k2tog, p4, k1, (p2, k1) 2 times, p6, yo, k2tog, k2.
Row 5: Sl 1, k3, yo, k2tog, (k1, yo) 2 times, k2tog, p1, ssk, p1, k2tog, p1, ssk, yo, k1, yo, k3, yo, k2tog, (yo twice, k2tog) 2 times, yo twice, k3—36 sts.
Row 6: K4, (p1, k2) 3 times, yo, k2tog, p5, (k1, p1) 2 times, k1, p7, yo, k2tog, k2.

Row 7: Sl 1, k3, yo, k2tog, k1, yo, k3, yo, sl 2tog k-wise, k1, p2sso, p1, sl 2tog k-wise, k1, p2sso, (yo, k3) 2 times, yo, k2tog, k11.
Row 8: BO 7, k5, yo, k2tog, p7, k1, p9, yo, k2tog, k2—29 sts.
Row 9: Sl 1, k3, yo, k2tog, k1, yo, k5, yo, sl 2tog k-wise, k1, p2sso, yo, k5, yo, k3, yo, k2tog, k4—31 sts.
Row 10: K6, yo, k2tog, p19, yo, k2tog, k2.

Finishing: Repeat Rows 1–10 for length desired.

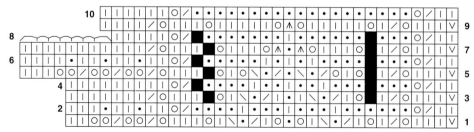

Repeat from Row 1 for length desired.

CO 31 sts. Knit 1 row.

THANK YOU AT THANKSGIVING

Every year at Thanksgiving I write a thank-you note to a person or business that I feel has performed a valuable service for me or others in the past year. One year I wrote to the Portuguese embassy in New York thanking them for Portugal's boneless and skinless sardines. The ambassador sent an enormous basket filled with every kind of sardine imaginable.

The family had sardines for a very long time.

Another year I wrote to the president of Union Bank. The local branch would send a representative to the Sunny View Lutheran Home where I lived to allow those of us who could not get out to do our banking. He sent me a large potted plant that I kept in my apartment.

Medallion Ground

Finished size: Repeat width 1 ¾", repeat interval 2 ¼".

Yarn: DMC Cebelia 5, (100% cotton; 130 m/50g): ecru.

Needles: Size 2 (2.8 mm).

Note: Sample shows 3 edge sts on each side.

CO a multiple of 24 + 1 sts. All even rows except 16, 18, 20, 36, 38, and 40: Purl. Rows 16, 18, 20, 36, 38 and 40: knit the purl sts from the row below.

Row 1: *K4, k2tog, yo, k1, yo, ssk, k3; repeat from *, end k1.

Row 3: *K3, k2tog, yo, k3, yo, ssk, k2; repeat from *, end k1.

Row 5: *K2, (k2tog, yo) 2 times, k1, (yo, ssk) 2 times, k1; repeat from *, end k1.

Row 7: K1, (k2tog, yo) 2 times, k3,

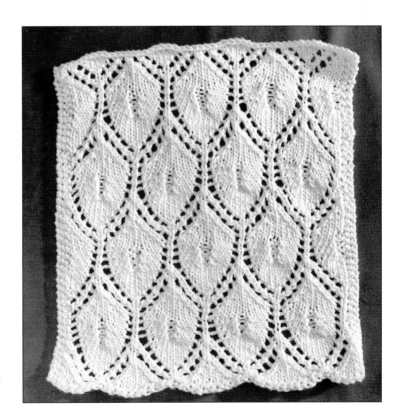

(yo, ssk) 2 times; repeat from *, end k1.

Row 9: (K2tog, yo) 2 times, k5, yo, ssk, yo, * sl 2tog k-wise, k1, p2sso, yo, k2tog, yo, k5, yo, ssk, yo; repeat from *, end last repeat k5 (yo, ssk) 2 times.

Row 11: *K1, k2tog, yo, k7, yo, ssk; repeat from *, end k1.

Row 13: K2tog, yo, k9, yo, * sl 2tog k-wise, k1, p2sso, yo, k9, yo; repeat from *, end last repeat k9, yo, ssk.

Row 15: *K1, yo, k3, ssk, p1, k2tog, k3, yo; repeat from *, end k1.

Row 17: *K1, yo, k3, ssk, p1, k2tog, k3, yo; repeat from *, end k1.

Row 19: *K1, yo, k3, ssk, p1, k2tog, k3, yo; repeat from *, end k1.

Row 21: *K1, yo, ssk, k7, k2tog, yo; repeat from *, end k1.

Row 23: *K2, yo, ssk, k5, k2tog, yo, k1; repeat from *, end k1.

Row 25: *K1, (yo, ssk) 2 times, k3, (k2tog, yo) 2 times; repeat from *, end k1.

Row 27: *K2, (yo, ssk) 2 times, k1, (k2tog, yo) 2 times, k1; repeat from *, end k1.

Row 29: *K3, yo, ssk, yo, sl 2tog k-wise, k1, p2sso, yo, k2tog, yo, k2; repeat from *, end k1.

Row 31: *K4, yo, ssk, k1, k2tog, yo, k3; repeat from *, end k1.

Row 33: *K5, yo, sl 2tog k-wise, k1, p2sso, yo, k4; repeat from *, end k1.

Row 35: *P1, k2tog, k3, yo, k1, yo, k3, ssk; repeat from *, end k1.

Row 37: *P1, k2tog, k3, yo, k1, yo, k3, ssk; repeat from *, end k1.

Row 39: *P1, k2tog, k3, yo, k1, yo, k3, ssk; repeat from *, end k1.

Row 40: P12, k1, *P11, k1; repeat from *, end k1.

Repeat rows 1–40 for length desired.

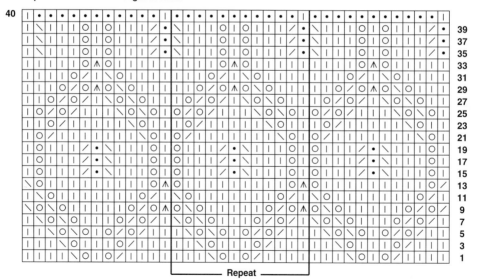

Repeat from Row 1 for length desired.

Even rows: Purl except rows 16, 18, 20, 36, 38, and 40, knit the purl sts from row below.

CO multiple of 24 sts + 1.

SUNNY VIEW LUTHERAN HOME

A few years ago I came to live at Sunny View Lutheran Home in Cupertino, California. People here are from many different places, but many of them are interested in handwork. I put up a notice that I would like to see knitted laces and maybe write the directions because I was trying to preserve and hand down patterns. I was offered several cherished and lovely patterns to record.

I have knitted altar laces for the chapel at Sunny View out of ecru linen. I used a pattern out of Marianne Kinzel's *Second Book of Modern Lace Knitting*.

Esther Sarlund's Doily

This doily was sent by Ester's mother from Finland around 1930. Esther treasured it so much that she kept it even after it got too tattered to display. But it was not in too bad a condition to translate.

Finished size: 14" diameter.

Yarn: DMC Cordonnet 30 (100% cotton; 197m/20g): white, 1 ball.
Needles: Size 0 (2.1 mm): set of 5 dpn.

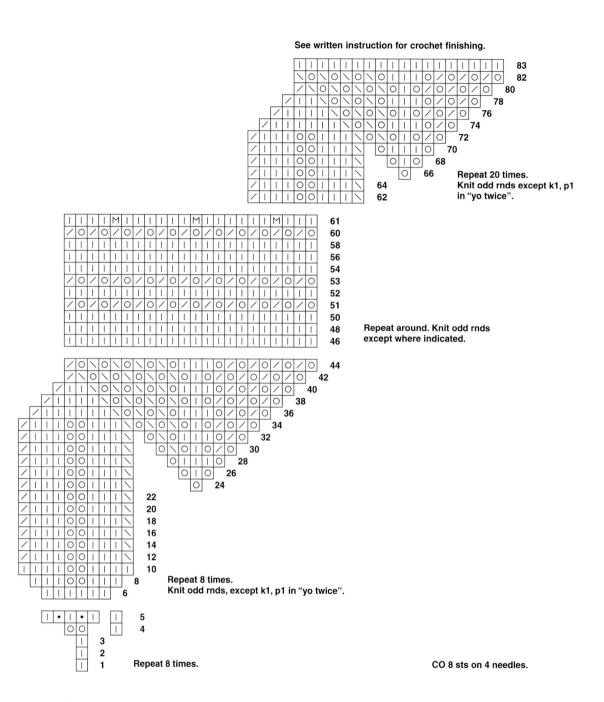

See written instruction for crochet finishing.

Repeat 20 times.
Knit odd rnds except k1, p1 in "yo twice".

Repeat around. Knit odd rnds except where indicated.

Repeat 8 times.
Knit odd rnds, except k1, p1 in "yo twice".

Repeat 8 times.

CO 8 sts on 4 needles.

Notions: Size 5 crochet hook.

CO 8 sts, 2 sts each on 4 needles. Repeat 8 times.

Rnd 1: Knit—8 sts.

Rnd 2: Knit.

Rnd 3: Knit.

Rnd 4: K1, yo twice—24 sts.

Rnd 5: K1, in the yo twice k1, p1, k1, p1, k1—48 sts.

Rnd 6: Knit.

Rnd 7: Knit.

Rnd 8: K3, yo twice, k3—64 sts.

Rnd 9: Knit all odd rounds, except k1, p1 in "yo twice".

Rnd 10: K4, yo twice, k4—80 sts.

Rnd 12: Ssk, k3, yo twice, k3, k2tog.

Rnd 14: Ssk, k3, yo twice, k3, k2tog.

Rnd 16: Ssk, k3, yo twice, k3, k2tog.

Rnd 18: Ssk, k3, yo twice, k3, k2tog.

Rnd 20: Ssk, k3, yo twice, k3, k2tog.

Rnd 22: Ssk, k3, yo twice, k3, k2tog.

Rnd 24: Yo, ssk, k3, yo twice, k3, k2tog—88 sts.

Rnd 26: Yo, k1, yo, ssk, k3, yo twice, k3, k2tog—104 sts.

Rnd 28: Yo, k3, yo, ssk, k3, yo twice, k3, k2tog—120 sts.

Rnd 30: Yo, k2tog, yo, k1, (yo, ssk) 2 times, k3, yo twice, k3, k2tog—136 sts.

Rnd 32: Yo, k2tog, yo, k3, (yo, ssk) 2 times, k3, yo twice, k3, k2tog—152 sts.

Rnd 34: (Yo, k2tog) 2 times, yo, k1, (yo, ssk) 3 times, k3, yo twice, k3, k2tog—168 sts.

Rnd 36: (Yo, k2tog) 2 times, yo, k3, (yo, ssk) 3 times, k6, k2tog.

Rnd 38: (Yo, k2tog) 3 times, yo, k1, (yo, ssk) 4 times, k4, k2tog.

Rnd 40: (Yo, k2tog) 3 times, yo, k3, (yo, ssk) 4 times, k2, k2tog.

Rnd 42: (Yo, k2tog) 4 times, yo, k1, (yo, ssk) 5 times, k2tog.

Rnd 44: (Yo, k2tog) 4 times, yo, k3, (yo, ssk) 4 times, yo, k2tog—176 sts.

Rnd 46: Knit.

Rnd 48: Knit.

Rnd 50: Knit.

Rnd 51: *Yo, k2tog; repeat from *.

Rnd 52: Knit.

Rnd 53: Yo, k2tog; repeat from *.

Rnd 54: Knit.

Rnd 56: Knit.

Rnd 58: Knit.

Rnd 60: *Yo, k2tog; repeat from *.

Rnd 61: *K3, knit in front and back, k6, knit in front and back, k6, knit in front and back, k4; repeat from *—200 sts.

Repeat 20 times. Odd rounds: Knit, except k1, p1 in "yo twice".

Rnd 62: Ssk, k3, yo twice, k3, k2tog—200 sts.

Rnd 64: Ssk, k3, yo twice, k3, k2tog.

Rnd 66: Yo, ssk, k3, yo twice, k3, k2tog—220 sts.

Rnd 68: Yo, k1, yo, ssk, k3, yo twice, k3, k2tog—260 sts.

Rnd 70: Yo, k3, yo, ssk, k3, yo twice, k3, k2tog—300 sts.

Rnd 72: Yo, k2tog, yo, k1, (yo, ssk) 2 times, k3, yo twice, k3, k2tog—340 sts.

Rnd 74: Yo, k2tog, yo, k3, (yo, ssk) 2 times, k6, k2tog.

Rnd 76: (Yo, k2tog) 2 times, yo, k1, (yo, ssk) 3 times, k4, k2tog.

Rnd 78: (Yo, k2tog) 2 times, yo, k3, (yo, ssk) 3 times, k2, k2tog.

Rnd 80: (Yo, k2tog) 3 times, yo, k1, (yo, ssk) 4 times, k2tog.

Rnd 82: (Yo, k2tog) 3 times, yo, k3, (yo, ssk) 4 times—360 sts.

Rnd 83: Knit.

With crochet hook, (sc through 3 sts, ch 7) around. Sl st to center of first loop, make a second and third round of loops.

Freda Frase's Small Doily

Freda purchased this doily at a white elephant sale around 1955. I don't think Freda could knit, but she could appreciate.

Finished Size: 7 ½" diameter.

Yarn: DMC Cebelia 10 (100% cotton; 260m/50g): white, 1 ball.

Needles: Size 2 (2.8 mm): set of 4 dpn.

Notions: Size 5 crochet hook.

Notes: Usually the rule is that when there has been a "yo twice" in the previous round, one must k1, p1 in the yos. This doily breaks that rule. In Rounds 23—30, the second yarn over is to be dropped, leaving one stitch on the needle to each "yo twice". One must drop the first yo then proceed with a k2tog or ssk as indicated by the directions.

CO 7 sts on 3 needles: 2 sts on needle 1, 2 sts on needle 2, 3 sts

on needle 3. All directions are repeated 7 times.

Rnd 1 and all odd rnds to Rnd 21: Knit.

Rnd 2: Yo, k1—2 sts—14 sts.

Rnd 4: (Yo, k1) 2 times—28 sts.

Rnd 6: (Yo, k2tog) 2 times.

Rnd 8: (Yo, k2) 2 times—42 sts.

Rnd 10: (Yo, k3) 2 times—56 sts.

Rnd 12: (Yo, k4) 2 times—70 sts.

Rnd 14: (Yo, k5) 2 times—84 sts.

Rnd 16: Yo, k12—91 sts.

Rnd 18: Yo, k5, sl 2tog k-wise, k1, p2sso, k5—84 sts.

Rnd 20: Yo, k1, yo, k4, sl 2tog k-wise, k1, p2sso, k4.

From Rnd 22 on: All rnds are pattern rnds.

Rnd 22: Yo, k3, yo, k9—98 sts.

Rnd 23: Yo twice, k2tog, yo, k1, yo, ssk, yo twice, k3, sl 2tog k-wise, k1, p2sso, k3—112 sts.

Rnd 24: Yo twice, k2tog, yo, k3, yo, ssk, yo twice, k7—126 sts.

Rnd 25: Yo twice, k2tog, yo, k5, yo, ssk, yo twice, k2, sl 2tog k-wise, k1, p2sso, k2.

Rnd 26: Yo twice, k2tog, yo, k7, yo, ssk, yo twice, k5—140 sts.

Rnd 27: Yo twice, k2tog, yo, k9, yo, ssk, yo twice, k1, sl 2tog k-wise, k1, p2sso, k1.

Rnd 28: Yo twice, k2tog, yo, k11, yo, ssk, yo twice, k3—154 sts.

Rnd 29: Yo twice, k2tog, yo, k13, yo, ssk, yo twice, sl 2tog k-wise, k1, p2sso.

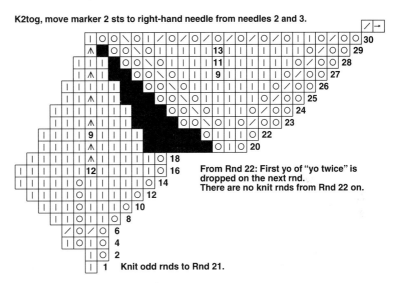

K2tog, move marker 2 sts to right-hand needle from needles 2 and 3.

From Rnd 22: First yo of "yo twice" is dropped on the next rnd.
There are no knit rnds from Rnd 22 on.

Knit odd rnds to Rnd 21.

CO 7 sts on 3 needles: 2 sts on needle 1, 2 sts on needle 2, 3 sts on needle 3.
Repeat directions 7 times.

Rnd 30: Yo twice, k2tog, yo, k2, (yo, k2tog) 6 times, k1, yo, ssk, yo twice, k1—168 sts.

Rnd 31: K2tog, move marker, then move 2 sts to the right-hand needle from needles 2 and 3. Yo, k17, yo, ssk, k1, k2tog—154 sts.

Rnd 32: Yo, k19, yo, sl 2tog k-wise, k1, p2sso.

Rnd 33: Yo, k21, yo, k1—168 sts. With crochet hook, sc through 3 sts, ch 6 around.

Freda Frase's Square Doily

Freda purchased this doily at the same white elephant sale around 1955.

Finished size: 9 ½" square.

Yarn: DMC Cebelia 10 (100% cotton; 260m/50g): white, 1 ball.

Needles: Size 2 (2.8 mm): set of 5 dpn.

Notions: Size E crochet hook.

CO 2 sts on each of 4 needles. Knit 1 rnd. Knit all even rnds unless directions indicate otherwise.

Repeat 4 times.

Rnd 1: K1, yo, k1—12 sts.

Rnd 3: (K1, yo) twice, k1—20 sts.

Rnd 5: Yo, k2, yo, k1, yo, k2—32 sts.

Rnd 7: (K1, yo, k3, yo) twice—48 sts.

Rnd 9: K1, yo, p1, k4, yo, k1, yo, k4, p1, yo—64 sts.

Rnd 10: K1, p2, k11, p2.

Rnd 11: K1, yo, p2, k5, yo, k1, yo, k5, p2, yo—80 sts.

Rnd 12: K1, p3, k13, p3.

Rnd 13: K1, yo, p3, k6, yo, k1, yo, k6, p3, yo—96 sts.

Rnd 14: K1, p4, k15, p4.

Rnd 15: K1, yo, p4, k15, p4, yo— 104 sts.

Rnd 16: K1, p5, k15, p5.

Rnd 17: K1, yo, p5, yo, ssk, k11, k2tog, yo, p5, yo—112 sts.

Rnd 18: K1, p7, k13, p7.

> ## *Mary's Teaching Notes*
> ## yo, p
> "Yo, p" requires two movements of the thread: 1) bring yarn forward then 2) wrap the thread completely around the needle. The thread ends up in front.

Rnd 19: K1, yo, p7, yo, ssk, k9, k2tog, yo, p7, yo—120 sts.

Rnd 20: K1, p9, k11, p9.

Rnd 21: K1, yo, p9, yo, ssk, k7, k2tog, yo, p9, yo—128 sts.

Rnd 22: K1, p11, k9, p11.

Rnd 23: K1, yo, p11, yo, ssk, k5, k2tog, yo, p11, yo—136 sts.

Rnd 24: K1, p13, k7, p13.

Rnd 25: K1, yo, p13, yo, ssk, k3, k2tog, yo, p13, yo—144 sts.

Rnd 26: K1, p15, k5, p15.

See written instruction for crochet finishing.

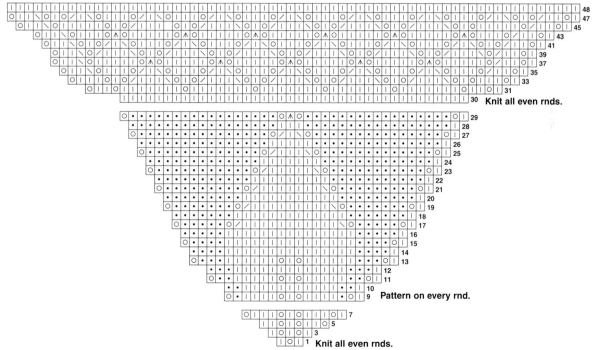

Knit all even rnds.

Pattern on every rnd.

Knit all even rnds.

Cast on 2 sts on each of 4 needles.
Knit 1 rnd.
Repeat chart 4 times.

Rnd 27: K1, yo, p15, yo, ssk, k1, k2tog, yo, p15, yo—152 sts.

Rnd 28: K1, p17, k3, p17.

Rnd 29: K1, yo, p17, yo, sl 2tog k-wise, k1, p2sso, yo, p17, yo—160 sts.

Rnd 30 and all rem even rnds: Knit.

Rnd 31: K1, yo, k2, yo, (k7, yo) 5 times, k2, yo—192 sts.

Rnd 33: K1, yo, k3, (yo, k1, yo, ssk, k3, k2tog) 5 times, yo, k1, yo, k3, yo—208 sts.

Rnd 35: K1, yo, k2, k2tog, (yo, k3, yo, ssk, k1, k2tog) 5 times, yo, k3, yo, ssk, k2, yo—216 sts.

Rnd 37: K1, yo, k2, k2tog, (yo, k5, yo, sl 2tog k-wise, k1, p2sso) 5 times, yo, k5, yo, ssk, k2, yo—224 sts.

Rnd 39: K1, yo, k2, k2tog, (yo, ssk, k3, k2tog, yo, k1) 5 times, yo, ssk, k3, k2tog, yo, ssk, k2, yo.

Rnd 41: K1, yo, k2, k2tog, yo, k1, (yo, ssk, k1, k2tog, yo, k3) 5 times, yo, ssk, k1, k2tog, yo, k1, yo, ssk, k2, yo—232 sts.

Rnd 43: K1, yo, k2, k2tog, yo, k3, (yo, sl 2tog k-wise, k1, p2sso, yo, k5) 5 times, yo, sl 2tog k-wise, k1, p2sso, yo, k3, yo, ssk, k2, yo—240 sts.

Rnd 45: K1, yo, k2, k2tog, yo, k5, (yo, k1, yo, ssk, k3, k2tog) 5 times, yo, k1, yo, k5, yo, ssk, k2, yo—256 sts.

Rnd 47: K1, yo, k2, k2tog, yo, k1, (yo, ssk, k1, k2tog, yo, k3) 6 times, yo, ssk, k1, k2tog, yo, k1, yo, ssk, k2, yo—264 sts.

Rnd 48: Knit.

Finishing: Move 1st from the right-hand needle to the left-hand needle. With crochet hook, (sc through 3 sts, chain 8) 4 times, (sc through 5 sts, chain 8, sc through 3 sts, chain 8) 6 times, (sc through 3 sts, chain 8) 2 times. Fasten off. Block to a perfect square.

LACE KNITTING CLASSES

In 1986 I taught a class in lace knitting. We did ten laces, one for each week of class. I selected the laces to teach progressively more challenging skills. All the laces for the class are included in this book if you'd like to try them.

Week 1. Very Narrow Lace. A good introduction to lace knitting.

Week 2. Serpentine Lace. Very easy. You can keep the pattern in mind. Double yos make a big hole.

Week 3. Shell Lace. Easy but not as easy as Serpentine Lace. Introduces witches' ladder.

Week 4. Cornwallis Lace. Nicest of the edgings. Combines three simpler patterns.

Week 5. Heirloom Apron Lace. My favorite. It's hard to make the diamond with a dot in the middle, then not put the dot in the next diamond. Uses two different versions of double decrease.

Week 6. Star Doily. Simple four-needle doily.

Week 7. Freda Frase's Small Doily. Introduces dropped stitches. It has only pattern rows, no knit rows after Row 20.

Week 8. Freda Frase's Square Doily. Five-needle doily. This is knitted in the round but turns out square.

Week 9. Christmas Star. The points use the technique of a knitted-on edge. They also introduce bias knitting.

Week 10. Esther Sarlund's Doily. Gives experience handling a large piece.

Serpentine Lace

This is a common, classic lace. The first time I saw it was when a Friend gave me a piece after church. She claimed the source to be old, and I have had it since around 1950.

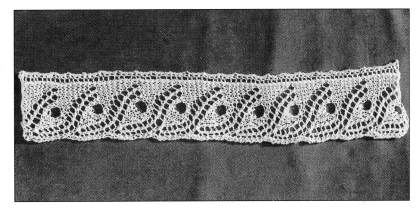

Finished size: Depth 1 ¾", repeat interval 1 ¼".

Yarn: DMC Cordonnet 30 (100% cotton; 197m/20g): white.

Needles: Size 1 (2.4 mm).

CO 18 sts. Knit 1 row.

Row 1: Sl 1, k1, yo, k2tog, k1, (yo, k2tog) 2 times, k1, yo 4 times, k2tog, k1, (yo, k2tog) 2 times, k1—21 sts.

Row 2: K7, (k1, p1, k1, p1) in "yo 4 times", k10.

Row 3: Sl 1, k1, yo, k2tog, k2, (yo, k2tog) 2 times, k5, (k2tog, yo) 2 times, k2.

Row 4 and all even rows: Knit.

Row 5: Sl 1, k1, yo, k2tog, k3, (yo, k2tog) 2 times, k4, (k2tog, yo) 2 times, k2.

Row 7: Sl 1, k1, yo, k2tog, k4, (yo, k2tog) 2 times, k1, k2tog, (k2tog, yo) 2 times, k2—20 sts.

Row 9: Sl 1, k1, yo, k2tog, k5, (yo, k2tog) 2 times, k1, (k2tog, yo) 2 times, k2.

Row 11: Sl 1, k1, yo, k2tog, k6, (yo,

K3tog, s1 back onto left needle and draw 1 st over it, replace k3tog st back on the right needle.

Repeat from Row 1 for length desired.

Row 4 and all even rows: Knit.

CO 18 sts. Knit 1 row.

k2tog) 2 times, (k2tog, yo) 2 times, k2.

Row 13: Sl 1, k1, yo, k2tog, k7, yo, k2tog, yo, k3tog, sl the last st made back onto left needle and draw 1 st over it, replace the k3tog st back on the right hand needle, yo, k2tog, k1—18 sts.

Row 15: Sl 1, k1, yo, k2tog, k8, yo, k2tog, yo, k1, k2tog, k1.

Row 16: Knit.

Finishing: Repeat Rows 1–16 for length desired.

PILLOWCASE EDGINGS

I have given away most of my knitted lace so others can appreciate it. I decided to make pillowcases with knitted edgings for each of my grandnieces and nephews as wedding gifts. But two or three of them all got married at the same time and I couldn't knit the edgings up fast enough. After that I decided to do as my Aunt Jennie did and knit the edgings up ahead of time. I made nineteen sets of pillowcase edgings. And I chuckle to myself every time I think that some won't get their gift from me until I've been dead for twenty years!

Leaf Lace

Pillowcases are 20" wide. A length of lace 40" is required for each pillowcase.

Finished size: Depth 2 ¼", repeat interval 1".

Yarn: DMC Cebelia 20, (100% cotton; 370m/50g): color 992.

Needles: Size 0 (2.1 mm).

CO 19 sts.

Set-up Row: K6, p2, k8, yo, k2tog, k1.

Row 1: Sl 1, k2, (yo, k2tog) 2 times, k3, k2tog, yo, k1, yo, ssk, yo, k4—20 sts.

Row 2: K6, p3, k8, yo, k2tog, k1.

Row 3: Sl 1, k2, (yo, k2tog)

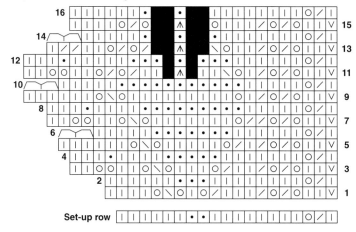

Repeat from Row 1 for length desired.

CO 19 sts.

Leaf Lace and Laura Brown's Rose Leaf.

2 times, k2, k2tog, yo, k3, yo, ssk, yo, k2, yo twice, k2—23 sts.

Row 4: K3, p1, k4, p5, k7, yo, k2tog, k1.

Row 5: Sl 1, k2, (yo, k2tog) 2 times, k1, k2tog, yo, k5, yo, ssk, yo, k6—24 sts.

Row 6: BO 2, k5, p7, k6, yo, k2tog, k1—22 sts.

Row 7: Sl 1, k2, (yo, k2tog) 2 times, k2tog, yo, k7, yo, ssk, yo, k2, yo twice, k2—25 sts.

Row 8: K3, p1, k4, p9, k5, yo, k2tog, k1.

Row 9: Sl 1, k2, (yo, k2tog) 2 times, k1, yo, k9, yo, ssk, yo, k6—27 sts.

Row 10: BO 2, k5, p11, k5, yo, k2tog, k1—25 sts.

Row 11: Sl 1, k2, (yo, k2tog) 2 times, k1, yo, ssk, k2, sl 2tog k-wise, k1, p2sso, k2, (k2tog, yo) 2 times, k2, yo twice, k2.

Row 12: K3, p1, k5, p7, k6, yo, k2tog, k1.

Row 13: Sl 1, k2, (yo, k2tog) 2 times, k2, yo, ssk, sl 2tog k-wise, k1, p2sso, (k2tog, yo) 2 times, k2, k2tog twice, k1—21 sts.

Row 14: BO 2, k5, p3, k7, yo, k2tog, k1—19 sts.

Row 15: Sl 1, k2, (yo, k2tog) 2 times, k3, yo, sl 2tog k-wise, k1, p2sso, yo, k2tog, yo, k4.

Row 16: K6, p2, k8, yo, k2tog, k1.

Finishing: Repeat Rows 1–16 for length desired.

LACY KNITTERS

By 1985, I had eight notebooks filled with patterns, plus half a dozen printed books. I began to search for a depository for my pattern collection without success. So few were interested in lacy knitting that it was rapidly becoming a lost art. I found a kindred soul in Gracie Larsen and, along with a few others, formed the Lacy Knitters. We began a pattern bank of which my collection represents the first 500 entries. The goal is to catalog lace knit patterns, check the patterns by knitting them, and, when not covered by copyright, make the patterns available to knitters. Even though I no longer knit, I attend meetings and answer questions.

I hope you will enjoy my patterns and that lace knitting shall not be a lost art.

Peacock Doily

This is one of the few pieces of knitting I still have in my possession. It is displayed on the back of my sofa. The pattern was published in Workbasket, *November 1954.*

Finished size: 12" square.
Yarn: DMC Cordonnet 30 (100% cotton; 197m/20g): white, 2 balls.
Needles: Size 0 (2.1 mm): set of 5 dpn, 21" circular.
Notions: Size 5 crochet hook, markers.

CO loosely 9 sts. Purl 1 row.
Row 1: Yo, k9—10 sts.
Row 2: Yo, p10—11 sts.
Row 3: Yo, k11—12 sts.
Row 4: Yo, p12—13 sts.
Row 5: Yo, k13—14 sts.
Row 6: Yo, p14—15 sts.
Row 7: Yo, k15—16 sts.
Row 8: Yo, p16—17 sts.
Rows 9, 11, 13, 15, and 17: Sl 1 k-wise, k16—17 sts.
Rows 10, 12, 14, 16, and 18: Sl 1 p-wise, p16—17 sts.
Row 19: Ssk, k2, yo, k2tog, k5, ssk, yo, k2, k2tog—15 sts.
Row 20: Sl 1 p-wise, p14.
Row 21: Ssk, k2, yo, k2tog, k4, ssk, yo, k1, k2tog—13 sts.
Row 22: Sl 1 p-wise, p12.
Row 23: Ssk twice, yo, k2tog, k3, ssk, yo, k2tog—10 sts.

Cut off thread, leaving a short length (after piece is completed weave in length of thread left from body along top of leg). This is the top needle, or neck. With another needle, pick up 9 sts down the side. With another needle pick up the 8 loops at the bottom that were made by casting on the 9 sts. With another needle pick up 9 sts on the last side to correspond with the first side. You will now have a space on each side of the 8 sts on the bottom needle. With the 5th needle and thread, holding the wrong side of the work toward you:

Rnd 1: Pick up and purl 3 sts in the space at right of bottom needle, p4 on bottom needle, yo, p4, pick up and purl 3 sts at left of needle, turn.
Rnd 2: Bottom needle: k7, yo, k1, yo, k7.
Side needle: (yo, p1) 5 times, turn.
Rnd 3: Side needle: k10.

Bottom needle: p8, k1, p8.

Side needle: (yo, k1) 5 times, turn.

Rnd 4: Side needle: k10, yo.

Bottom needle: k2tog, k4, ssk, yo, k1, yo, k2tog, k4, ssk.

Side needle: yo, k10, (yo, k1) 3 times, turn.

Rnd 5: Side needle: k17.

Bottom needle: p7, k1, p7.

Side needle: k11, (yo, k1) 4 times, turn.

Rnd 6: Side needle: k19, yo.

Bottom needle: k2tog, k3, ssk, yo, k1, yo, k2tog, k3, ssk.

Side needle: yo, k17, yo, k1.

Top needle: ssk, k8. Continue on next needle without turning.

Side needle: p20.

Bottom needle: k6, p1, k6. Continue.

Rnd 7: Side needle: p2, (yo, k3) 4 times, (yo, k2) 3 times, yo, pick up and knit 2 sts—30 sts on needle.

Top needle: yo, k3tog through back of sts, k3, k3tog through front of sts.

Side needle: (yo, k2) 3 times, (yo, k3) 4 times, yo, k2.

Bottom needle: yo, k2tog, k2, ssk, yo, k1, yo, k2tog, k2, ssk.

Side needle: yo, k2, sl to bottom needle.

Rnd 8: Side needle: k28, sl last 9 sts made to empty needle and continue.

Top needle: k6 with same top needle, k7 from side needle.

Side needle: k19, p2, sl last 2 sts to empty needle and continue on bottom needle, p1, k5, p1, k5, p3. There are now 19 sts on each side needle, 22 sts on top, 17 sts on bottom.

Rnd 9: Side needle: (yo, k4) 2 times, (yo, k2tog, k2) 2 times, yo, k3.

Top needle: (yo, k3) 3 times, yo, k2tog, k3, ssk, (yo, k3) 2 times, yo.

Side needle: k3, (yo, k2, ssk) 2 times, yo, k3, turn. Purl all 15 sts just worked on side needle and the 27 sts on top needle.

On next side needle: p16, turn.

Rnd 10: Side needle: k4, (yo, k4) 3 times.

Top needle: (yo, k4) 3 times, yo, k2tog, k4, yo, k1, (yo, k4) 2 times, yo.

Side needle: k4, yo, k2, ssk, yo, k2, turn. P11 sts just worked and all sts on top needle.

Third needle: p14, turn.

Rnd 11 Side needle: k4, (yo, k2tog, k3) 2 times.

Top needle: (yo, k2tog, k3) 3 times, yo, k4, ssk, yo, k1, k2tog, yo, (k3, ssk, yo) 2 times.

Side needle: k3, ssk, yo, k4, turn. Purl 2 needles.

Side needle: p9, turn.

Rnd 12: Side needle: k4, yo, k5.

Top needle: (yo, k5) 3 times, yo, k2tog, k4, yo, k2tog, k2, yo, (k5, yo) 2 times.

Side needle: k4, turn, p4.

Top needle: p41.

Side needle: p5, turn.

Rnd 13: Side needle: k5.

Top needle: (yo, k2tog, k4) 3 times, yo, k2tog, k2, ssk, yo, k2tog, k3, yo, (k4, ssk, yo) 2 times.

Side needle: k5, (yo, k4) 4 times, yo.

Bottom needle: k3, yo, k2tog, k1, ssk, yo, k1, yo, k2tog, k1, ssk, yo, k3.

Rnd 14: Side needle: k26.

Top needle: k41.

Side needle: k26.

Bottom needle: p4, k3, p3, k3, p4.

Rnd 15: Side needle: (yo, k1, k2tog, yo, k2) 4 times, yo, k2tog twice, yo, k2.

Top needle: (yo, k2tog twice, yo, k2) 3 times, yo, k3, ssk, yo, k1, k2tog, yo, k2tog, k1, yo, (k2, yo, ssk twice, yo) 2 times.

Side needle: k2, yo, ssk twice, yo, (k2, yo, ssk, k1, yo) 4 times.

Bottom needle: k4, yo, k3tog through back of sts, yo, k3, yo, k3tog through back of sts, yo, k4.

Rnd 16: Side needle: p1, k29.

Top needle: k42.

Side needle: k29, p1.

Bottom needle: p4, k3, p3, k3, p4.

Sl 1 st from each side needle to bottom needle. With front of work facing you and the top nee-dle on top, take 1 st from right of top needle to right side needle and 3 sts from left of top needle to left side needle.

Rnd 17: Side needle: yo, (k2tog, k1, k2tog, yo, k1, yo) 5 times.

Top needle: (k2tog, k1, k2tog, yo, k1, yo) 3 times, k2, ssk, yo twice, ssk, k2tog twice, (yo, k1, yo, ssk, k1, k2tog) 2 times.

Side needle: (yo, k1, yo, ssk, k1, k2tog) 5 times, yo.

Bottom needle: k5, yo, k3tog through back of sts, yo, k3, yo, k3tog through back of sts, yo, k5.

Rnd 18: Side needle: k31.

Top needle: k22, p1, k15.

Side needle: k31.

Bottom needle: p5, k3, p3, k3, p5.

Rnd 19: Side needle: yo, k1, yo, k3tog, (yo, k2tog, yo, k1, yo, k3tog) 4 times, yo, k2tog, yo, k1.

Top needle: yo, k3tog, (yo, k2tog, yo, k1, yo, k3tog) 2 times, yo, k2tog, yo, k2tog, k4, yo twice, k3tog, (yo, k1, yo, ssk, yo, k3tog) 2 times, yo.

Side needle: k1, (yo, ssk, yo, k3tog, yo, k1) 5 times, yo.

Bottom needle: k5, yo, k3tog through back of sts, yo, k3, yo, k3tog through back of sts, yo, k5.

Rnd 20: Side needle: k32.

Top needle: k23, p1, k14.

Side needle: k32.

Bottom needle: p5, k3, p3, k3, p5, yo.

Rnd 21: Side needle: (k2tog, k4, yo) 5 times, k2tog.

Top needle: k4, yo, (k2tog, k4, yo) 2 times, k2tog, k6, yo, k2, ssk, yo, k4, ssk, yo, k4.

Side needle: ssk, (yo, k4, ssk) 5 times.

Bottom needle: yo, k5, yo, k3tog through back of sts, yo, k3, yo, k3tog through back of sts, yo, k6.

Rnd 22: Side needle: k31.

Top needle: k39.

Side needle: k31.

Bottom needle: p6, k3, p3, k3, p6.

Rnd 23: Side needle: yo, k5, (yo, k6) 4 times, yo, k2.

Top needle: k4, (yo, k6) 2 times, yo, k2tog, k1, yo, k2tog, for bill: work next 3 sts thus: sl first st p-wise, bind the third st over the second, return first slipped st to left needle and bind second st over first, then k the first st; yo, k5, yo, k6, yo, k4.

Side needle: k2, yo, (k6, yo) 4 times, k5, yo.

Bottom needle: k6, yo, k3tog through the back of sts, yo, k3, yo, k3tog through the back of sts, yo, k6.

Rnd 24: Side needle: k37.

Top needle: k42.

Side needle: k37.

Bottom needle: p6, k3, p3, k3, p6, yo.

Rnd 25: Side needle: k6, (yo, k2tog, k5) 4 times, yo, k2tog, k1.

Top needle: k4, (yo, k2tog, k5) 2 times, yo, k1, yo, k2tog, k1, ssk, yo, k1, yo, k6, yo, k5, ssk, yo, k4.

Side needle: k1, ssk, yo, (k5, ssk, yo) 4 times, k6.

Bottom needle: yo, k6, yo, k3tog through back of sts, yo, k3, yo, k3tog through back of sts, yo, k7.

Rnd 26: Side needle: k37, then on same side needle, k11 sts from top needle.

Top needle: k7, p3, k3, p3, k18, then sl last 11 knit sts to empty needle and continue on side needle, k37.

Bottom needle: p7, k3, p3, k3, p7.

Rnd 27: Side needle: yo, k6, (yo, k7) 6 times.

Top needle: yo, k7, yo, k2tog, k1, yo, k3tog, yo, k1, ssk, yo, k7, yo.

Side needle: (k7, yo) 6 times, k6, yo.

Bottom needle: k7, yo, k3tog through back of sts, yo, k3, yo, k3 through back of sts, yo, k7.

Rnd 28: Side needle: k55.

Top needle: k9, p4, k1tbl, p4, k8.

Side needle: k55.

Bottom needle: p7, k3, p3, k3, p7, yo.

Rnd 29: Side needle: k1, yo, ssk, k1, k2tog, yo, k1, (yo, k2tog, k6) 6 times.

Top needle: yo, k2tog, k6, yo, k2tog twice, yo, k1tbl, yo, ssk twice, yo, k6, ssk, yo.

Side needle: (k6, ssk, yo) 6 times, k1, yo, ssk, k1, k2tog, yo, k1.

Bottom needle: yo, k7, yo, k3tog through the back of sts, yo, k3, yo, k3tog through back of sts, yo, k8.

Rnd 30: Side needle: k55.

Top needle: k8, p2, k5, p2, k8.

Side needle: k55.

Bottom needle: p8, k3, p3, k3, p8, yo.

Rnd 31: Side needle: ssk, yo, k3tog, yo, k2tog, (yo, k1) 2 times, yo, ssk, k1, k2tog, yo, k1, (yo, k8) 5 times.

Top needle: yo, k8, yo, k1, k2tog, yo, k3, yo, ssk, k1, yo, k8, yo.

Side needle: (k8, yo) 5 times, k1, yo, ssk, k1, k2tog, (yo, k1) 2 times, yo, ssk, yo, k3tog, yo, k2tog.

Bottom needle: yo, k8, yo, k3 through back of sts, yo, k3, yo, k3tog through back of sts, yo, k9.

Rnd 32: Side needle: k1, k2tog, k2, p3, k52.

Top needle: k9, p2, k7, p2, k9.

Side needle: k52, p3, k1, k2tog, k2.

Bottom needle: p9, k3, p3, k3, p9, yo.

Rnd 33: Side needle: ssk, k2tog, yo, k3, yo, ssk, yo, k3tog, yo, k2tog, yo, k1, (yo, ssk) 2 times, k1, k2tog, yo, k1, (yo, k2tog, k7) 4 times.

Top needle: yo, k2tog, k7, yo, k1, (k2tog, yo) 2 times, k1tbl, (yo, ssk) 2 times, k1, yo, k7, ssk, yo.

Side needle: (k7, ssk, yo) 4 times, k1, yo, ssk, k1, k2tog, yo, k2tog, yo, k1, yo, ssk, yo, k3tog, yo, k2tog, yo, k3, yo, ssk, k2tog.

Bottom needle: yo, k8, k2tog, yo, k1tbl, ssk, k1, k2tog, yo, k1tbl, yo, ssk, k8, k1 and p1 in last st.

Rnd 34: Side needle: k2tog, k1 and p1 in next st, p4, k1, k2tog, k2, p3, k43.

Top needle: k9, p2, k9, p2, k9.

Side needle: k43, p3, k1, k2tog, k2, p4, p1 and k1 in next st, k2tog.

Bottom needle: k1 and p1 in next st, p8, k5, p1, k5, p10.

Rnd 35: Side needle: k7, yo, ssk, k2tog, yo, k3, yo, ssk, yo, k3tog, yo, k2tog, yo, k1, (yo, ssk) 2 times, k1, k2tog, yo, k1, (yo, k9) 3 times.

Top needle: yo, k9, yo, k1, (k2tog, yo) 2 times, k3, (yo, ssk) 2 times, k1, yo, k9, yo.

Side needle: (k9, yo) 3 times, k1, yo, ssk, k1, (k2tog, yo) 2 times, k1, yo, ssk, yo, k3tog, yo, k2tog, yo, k3, yo, ssk, k2tog, yo, k7.

Bottom needle: k9, k2tog, yo, k3, yo, k3tog, yo, k3, yo, ssk, k9.

Rnd 36: Side needle: p7, p1 and k1 in next st, k2tog, k1 and p1 in next st, p4, k1, k2tog, k2, p3, k37.

Top needle: k10, p2, k11, p2, k10.

Side needle: k37, p3, k1, k2tog, k2, p4, p1 and k1 in next st, ssk, k1 and p1 in next st, p7.

Bottom needle: p9, k1, p11, k1, p9.

Rnd 37: Side needle: k16, yo, ssk, k2tog, yo, k3, yo, ssk, yo, k3tog, yo, k2tog, (yo, k1, yo, ssk, yo, ssk, k1, k2tog, yo, k2tog) 3 times.

Top needle: yo, k1, (yo, ssk) 2 times, k1, (k2tog, yo) 2 times, k3, (k2tog, yo) 2 times, k1tbl, (yo, ssk) 2 times, k3, (yo, ssk) 2 times, k1, (k2tog, yo) 2 times, k1, yo.

Side needle: (ssk, yo, ssk, k1, k2tog, yo, k2tog, yo, k1, yo) 3 times, ssk, yo, k3tog, yo, k2tog, yo, k3, yo, ssk, k2tog, yo, k16.

Bottom needle: k8, yo, k2tog, yo, k5, yo, k1tbl, yo, k5, yo, ssk, yo, k8.

Rnd 38: Side needle: p16, p1 and k1 in next st, k2tog, k1 and p1 in next st, p4, k1, k2tog, k2, (p3, k7) 3 times.

Top needle: p3, k7, p6, k5, p6, k7, p3.

Side needle: (k7, p3) 3 times, k1, k2tog, k2, p4, p1 and k1 in next st, k2tog, k1 and p1 in next st, p16.

Bottom needle: p35.

Rnd 39: Side needle: k25, yo, ssk, k2tog, (yo, k3, yo, ssk, yo, k3tog, yo, k2tog) 3 times.

Top needle: yo, k3, yo, ssk, yo, k3tog, yo, k2tog, yo, k5, k2tog, yo, k3, yo, ssk, k5, yo, ssk, yo, k3tog, yo, k2tog, yo, k3, yo.

Side needle: (ssk, yo, k3tog, yo, k2tog, yo, k3, yo) 3 times, ssk, k2tog, yo, k25.

Bottom needle: k35.

Rnd 40: Side needle: p25, p1 and k1 in next st, k2tog, k1 and p1 in next st, p4, k1, k2tog, k2, (p5, k1, k2tog, k2) 2 times.

Top needle: P5, k1, k2tog, k2, p19, k1, k2tog, k2, p5.

Side needle: (k1, k2tog, k2, p5) 2 times, k1, k2tog, k2, p4, p1 and k1 in next st, k2tog, k1 and p1 in next st, p25.

Bottom needle: p35.

Rnd 41: Side needle: k34, yo, ssk, k2tog, (yo, k5, yo, ssk, k2tog) 2 times.

Top needle: yo, k5, yo, ssk, k2tog, yo, k19, yo, ssk, k2tog, yo, k5, yo.

Side needle: (ssk, k2tog, yo, k5, yo) 2 times, ssk, k2tog, yo, k34.

Bottom needle: k35.

Rnd 42: Side needle: p34, (p1 and k1 in next st, k2tog, k1 and p1 in next st, p5) 2 times, p1 and k1 in next st, k2tog.

Top needle: k1 and p1 in next st, p5, p1 and k1 in next st, k2tog, k1 and p1 in next st, p19, p1 and k1 in next st, ssk, k1 and p1 in next st, p5, p1 and k1 in next st.

Side needle: (ssk, p6, p1 and k1 in next st) 2 times, ssk, k1 and p1 in next st, p34.

Bottom needle: p35.

Rnd 43: Knit—190 sts.

Rnd 44: Purl.

Rnd 45: Knit.

Rnd 46: Purl.

Rnd 47: K2tog at beginning of each side needle, knit each st around—188 sts.

Rnd 48: Knit.

Rnd 49: Yo, k2tog, repeat around.

Rnd 50: Knit.

Rnd 51: Yo, k2tog, repeat around.

Rnd 52: Knit.

Rnd 53: Yo, k2tog, repeat around.

Rnd 54: Knit.

Rnd 55: Yo, k2tog, repeat around.

Rnd 56: Knit.

Rnd 57: Knit.

Rnd 58: Knit.

Rearrange sts on needles until you have 47 sts on each needle. Use a starting marker for first st of each rnd. Be sure your starting marker always has the peacock exactly square in center of the 47 sts on each needle—center of peacock top and bottom should be over the 24th st of top and bottom needles.

In all remaining rnds the directions are given for 1 needle and must be repeated for each of the other needles.

Rnd 59: Yo, k46, yo, k1—49 sts.

Rnd 60: Knit.

Rnd 61: Yo, k48, yo, k1—51 sts.

Rnd 62: K1, p1 in yo of previous rnd, k48, k1, p1 in yo of previous rnd, k1—53 sts.

Rnd 63: Yo, k52, yo, k1—55 sts.

Rnd 64: K1, p1 in yo of previous rnd, k52, k1, p1 in yo of previous rnd, k1—57 sts.

Rnd 65: Yo, k56, yo, k1—59 sts.

Rnd 66: K1, p1 in yo of previous rnd, k56, k1, p1 in yo of previous rnd, k1—61 sts.

Rnd 67: Yo, k60, yo, k1—63 sts.

Rnd 68: K1, p1 in yo of previous rnd, k60, k1, p1 in yo of previous rnd, k1—65 sts.

Rnd 69: Yo, k64, yo, k1—67 sts.

Rnd 70: Knit.

Rnd 71: Sl 1 from right to left needle before beginning this rnd. (Yo, k2tog) 32 times, yo, k3tog—66 sts.

Rnd 72: Knit.

Rnd 73: (Yo, k2tog) 33 times.

Rnd 74: Knit.

Rnd 75: Yo twice, k2tog, (yo, k2tog) 31 times, yo twice, k2tog—68 sts.

Rnd 76: (K1, p1) in "yo twice" of previous rnd, k63, (k1, p1) in "yo twice" of previous rnd, k1.

Rnd 77: K1, (yo, k2tog) 33 times, k1.

Rnd 78: Knit.

Rnd 79: K1, (yo, k2tog) 33 times, k1 and p1 in the last st—69 sts.

Rnd 80: Knit.

Rnd 81: Yo, k3, yo, (k2tog, k4, k2tog, yo, k1, yo) 6 times, k2tog, k4, k2tog, yo, k3, yo, k1—71 sts.

Rnd 82 and all even rnds through 98: Knit.

Rnd 83: K1, yo, k3, yo, (k2tog, k4, k2tog, yo, k1, yo) 6 times, k2tog, k4, k2tog, yo, k3, yo, k2—73 sts.

Rnd 85: K2, yo, k3, yo, (k2tog, k4, k2tog, yo, k1, yo) 6 times, k2tog, k4, k2tog, (yo, k3) 2 times—75 sts.

Rnd 87: (Yo, k3) 2 times, yo, (k2tog, k4, k tog, yo, k1, yo) 6 times, k tog, k4, k2tog, (yo, k3) 2 times, yo, k1—79 sts.

Rnd 89: K1, yo, k4, yo, k3, yo, (k2tog, k4, k2tog, yo, k1, yo) 6 times, k2tog, k4, k2tog, yo, k3, yo, k4, yo, k2—83 sts.

Rnd 91: K2, yo, k3, k2tog, yo, k3, yo, (k2tog, k4, k2tog, yo, k1, yo) 6 times, k2tog, k4, k2tog, yo, k3, yo, k2tog, k3, yo, k3—85 sts.

Rnd 93: (Yo, k3) 2 times, k2tog, yo, k3, yo, (k2tog twice, yo, k2tog twice, yo, k1, yo) 6 times, k2tog twice, yo, k2tog twice, yo, k3, yo, k2tog, (k3, yo) 2 times, k1—82 sts.

Rnd 95: K1, yo, k4, yo, k3, k2tog, yo, k3, yo, k1, yo, (k2tog, k1, k2tog, yo, k1, yo, k1, yo, k1, yo) 6 times, k2tog, k1, k2tog, yo, k1, yo, k3, yo, k2tog, k3, yo, k4, yo, k2—100 sts.

Rnd 97: K2, (yo, k3, k2tog) 2 times, (yo, k3) 2 times, (yo, k3tog, yo, k7) 6 times, yo, k3tog, yo, (k3, yo) 2 times, (k2tog, k3, yo) 2 times, k3—104 sts.

Rnd 98: Knit.

•**Edge:** Move starting marker one st to left. *Pick up next 3 sts with crochet hook and sc through all sts. Ch 7. Pick up the following number of sts: 2, 5, 5, 3, 4, (3, 2) 14 times, 3, 4, 3, 2, always with ch 7 between. Repeat from * around.

Finishing: Block to a true square.

Abbreviations

beg	begin(ning)
BO	bind off
ch	chain
CO	cast on
cont	continue
inc	knit in front and back of st
k	knit
k-wise	as to knit
p	purl
p-wise	as to purl
patt	pattern
psso	pass slipped stitch over
rem	remain(ing)
rep	repeat
rnd	round
sc	single crochet
sl	slip
ssk	slip, slip, knit 2 slipped sts tog
st(s)	stitch(es)
tbl	through back loop
tog	together
wyib	with yarn in back
yo	yarn over

Chart Symbols

□	Knit
○	yarn over
╱	k2tog
╲	ssk
⋀	centered double decrease— sl 2tog k-wise, k1, p2sso
↖	k3tog tbl for left slant
↗	k3tog for tight slant
•	purl
╱•	p2tog
╲•	p2tog tbl
⋊	p3tog
∨	sl 1wyib
⌢	bind off
↧	k1, p1 in st
↧	k2, p1, k1 in st
→	slip st in direction of arrow
▣	special st, see individual patterns
M	make 1. K in front and back of st
12	numbers within charts indicate number of k sts in row
▨	no stitch

INDEX